THE **KOGAN PAGE GUIDE** TO

WORKING IN ARTS, CRAFTS AND DESIGN

THE KOGAN PAGE GUIDE TO

WORKING IN ARTS, CRAFTS AND DESIGN

SECOND EDITION

Edited by
David Shacklady

**KOGAN
PAGE**

First published as *The Kogan Page Guide to Careers in Arts, Crafts and Design*, 1989
This second edition published 1997

Apart from any fair dealing for the purposes of research or private study, or criticism or review, as permitted under the Copyright, Designs and Patents Act 1988, this publication may only be reproduced, stored or transmitted, in any form or by any means, with the prior permission in writing of the publishers, or in the case of reprographic reproduction in accordance with the terms of licences issued by the Copyright Licensing Agency. Enquiries concerning reproduction outside those terms should be sent to the publishers at the undermentioned address:

Kogan Page Limited
120 Pentonville Road
London N1 9JN

© Kogan Page 1997

British Library Cataloguing in Publication Data

A CIP record for this book is available from the British Library.

ISBN 0 7494 2138 X

Typeset by Kogan Page Ltd
Printed and bound in Great Britain by Clays Ltd, St Ives plc

Contents

Acknowledgements

The editor has referred to the following Kogan Page publications in the preparation of this book: *Careers in Art and Design*, Linda Ball and Noel Chapman; *Careers in Fashion*, Noel Chapman; *Careers in Film and Video*, Noel Chapman; *Careers in Marketing, Advertising and Public Relations* Caroline Hird and Joanne Grigg; *Careers in Publishing and Bookselling*, June Lines; *Careers in the Theatre*, Jean Richardson; *Careers in Teaching*, Felicity Taylor; *Careers in Television and Radio*, Michael Selby. Also thanks to Alison King and Rachel for their support.

Introduction

There is a saying: 'art for art's sake, money for God's sake.' It could be a strap line for this book. Any reader considering a career in the creative professions within its covers should know that, for the most part, employment in these areas requires abilities or aptitudes that are not necessarily creative. You may be required to obtain technical or business skills. You will almost certainly be required to work to very specific briefs and to tight deadlines. With the exception of those at the very top of these professions, there may be much more of a necessity to compromise than create and to work as a member of a team rather than as an inspired individual. Applying your talents to the industry in which you wish to work will bring both job satisfaction and financial reward.

The scope of this book is very wide. It should be used as a general first reference point for those deciding on which career is most suitable. No one chapter is completely self-contained; all are extensively cross-referenced. The presentation is aimed at easy reference. The chapters are divided into career areas, within which the jobs are described and a next point of contact included for further information. Under each job heading a section on training is included. For the design jobs which require an art school qualification readers will be referred to Chapter 2 and the section on Education for Art and Design (pages 11–16), and to Table 1 (pages 14–15) and Figure 1 (page 16). There are other books in the Kogan Page series *Careers in* which cover the individual areas in more depth and contain case studies of those working in the professions and useful extra insights.

Making Yourself a Quality Applicant

Almost all the jobs contained within this book are extremely competitive at the recruitment stage. For many, entry on to specific education courses, which do not guarantee a job on completion, are also competitive. For example, the applications for film, radio and film degrees runs at an average of 15 people per place. Even at the lower level of local foundation courses there are many more applicants than places.

Does this mean you should give up now? Definitely not! You have made a start by beginning to inform yourself about the industries you are interested in. What you need to do is become a *quality applicant*. This will require: gaining a clear idea of what you want to do; long-term planning in terms of the route you will take; and a willingness to make a personal commitment to further your ambitions by picking up unpaid or voluntary work in your chosen field. It will be those who do the right things at the right time and take advice who will be most likely to succeed rather than those who are just simply 'brilliant' in their chosen field.

It may be useful to follow the action plan below.

1. Focus on the Career Area

Begin with this book. Sort out your ideas on a careers area. Follow up the addresses in Further Information. Find out as much as you can from any source. See if you can visit a practitioner in the field you are looking at. He or she may give you useful insights or put you off completely.

2. Educational/Training Route

Your research should have indicated educational or training routes that are traditionally followed to employment. Be clear about the requirements. It would be useful to contact your local careers service if you are under 19, or your local Adult Guidance Service. They will be able to advise you of qualification routes and local provision. Take their advice. They deal with hundreds of people a year seeking to get into the arts. They will also give you access to a comprehensive careers library.

3. Applying for Courses, Traineeships, Jobs

There are usually recruitment calendars for colleges or employers. Find out what these are. For most art school HND/Degree courses it is essential to apply by 15 December prior to the year of entry. For foundation courses it is also recommended to put in your application early as course places are filled on a first come first served basis. Contact the employers you are interested in to find out when they recruit. Look in the appropriate professional journals or trade magazines. It may be that you have to wait until the next yearly round.

4. Gaining Experience

As many of the courses and employers in these areas are not lacking in applicants they will look to recruit those who have shown some additional commitment. You can show this through: relevant voluntary work, such as at a local radio station; personal projects, such as video films made for competitions, clothes made for yourself; participation in cultural activities, such as being involved with local theatre groups.

5. Making Your Applications

It is important to realise that all these industries are presentation industries. The quality of your application will be scrutinised. If you need to present a portfolio then take advice from an art teacher, or if you are a mature student, find a portfolio preparation course at your local Adult Education Institute. Make full use of the experience you have gained and the skills you can demonstrate. Again, take advice from careers service professionals. Always get someone to proofread your applications

6. Interviews

If you get to the interview stage for a course or employer, make sure you are well prepared both about what you are applying for and the college/organisation/company to which you are applying. If possible, get someone to give you a mock interview.

Following this action plan will not only dramatically increase your chances of success but also ensure that you make the right decision for the right reasons. It is undoubtedly true that many of those applying for the highly competitive professions contained in this book will be rejected because they only have some vague notion of, or attraction to, the course/employment they are applying for or are not sufficiently prepared to express their suitability.

Employee or Freelance?

As the employment market in the UK changes, there are more and more people in all professions on freelance or short-term contracts. This has always been a feature of employment in art, craft and design industries. Sometimes people start as employees in an industry and, after gaining experience and contacts, set themselves up on a freelance basis or with their own business. Sometimes it is a necessity, as in interior design. Often groups of designers or artists will come together to share offices or workshops and contacts. If you plan to do this then you need to become informed about your rights and obligations, and take advice on tax, insurance and pensions (see *Working for Yourself: The Daily Telegraph Guide to Self Employment* (15th edition) by Godfrey Golzen).

Entry Requirements and Training – General

Most of the jobs in this book require the completion of higher education courses. This is a sign both of the competitive nature of the occupations, which allow recruitment of 'the best' even to the most menial of first jobs, and the increasing numbers of those acquiring higher educational qualifications.

Currently, 26 per cent of young people are going on to university. By the year 2000 this should be 30 per cent. There is also the expectation that people will be involved in lifelong learning which will mean returning to education to update skills as the new technologies revolutionise even these creative industries.

Art and design also has its own unique educational routes. These are described in Chapter 2. It is important for those considering applying to art schools to understand that one of these unique routes – the foundation course – is almost a statutory requirement (see page 12).

Training on the job will increasingly be through National Vocational Qualifications which are assessments of competencies in the workplace and use portfolios of work to make awards.

Employment Outlook

Having emphasised in this introduction the competitive nature of art and design, it is appropriate to end it with some facts and figures about prospects. In 1996, 7,460 people graduated in art and design subjects. Of those entering employment, 56 per cent found work in entertainment and creative work, another 10 per cent found work in teaching and lecturing, with 6 per cent finding work in retail, marketing and buying. Of the total graduating, 5 per cent went on to teacher training courses (source: *What Graduates Do?,* 1996, published by the Association of Graduate Careers Advisory Services (AGCAS)).

Good luck and good reading.

David Shacklady
December 1996

Chapter 1

Advertising

What is Advertising?

Advertising is defined by the *Oxford Dictionary* as: 'making generally or publicly known'; 'describing goods publicly with a view to increasing sales'; and 'to notify'. All advertisements attempt to reach a target audience. This may be to encourage an action, usually the purchase of a product. However, only 40 per cent of advertising expenditure is concerned with persuading people to buy. It is otherwise used to raise the profile of an organisation or industry. This may be to raise money for charities or to secure votes in an election. It may be to offer information for the public good. This may be in the form of campaigns for road safety or public health. It may simply be to fill jobs. What each attempts to do is to emphasise to a target audience the clear benefits of its product or service.

We will concentrate here on the activities of advertising agencies since although organisations often run their own campaigns, either because they are too small to buy in consultancy services or because they are large enough to have their own advertising departments, the principles and techniques can be more clearly seen through what an agency does. The main advertising agencies are based in London, although there are some in other large cities in Great Britain.

The Advertising Agency

An agency offers a service to organisations wanting to distribute information about their product or service. It employs a combination of people with specific roles. As this book is mainly concerned with the creative side of advertising, it is worth noting that in agencies the creative people may be outnumbered by three to one by: *account executives* who will be the link between the client and the advertising agency; *media executives* and *buyers* who will choose the channel of communication and purchase the advertising space or air time; and *market researchers* who will provide statistical analysis of the target audience and its perceptions. The creative process is very much at the end of the line. In fact, the campaign theme, medium and message will already have been determined before the creative work begins. The creative team will therefore be working to a very tight brief.

The Creative Department

This is where the ideas and plans are translated into visual images and words. There will be various people assigned, often in teams, to various accounts. Often these creative posts will be offered on a freelance basis to copywriters and art directors suited to the job in hand.

Agency Producers

These people are responsible for the production of a television or film advertisement. This is very much like making a mini-film. In fact, if a client is spending a great deal of money (for a car, for example), the sum involved has been known to cost more than an entire feature film. The agency producer will invariably work with an outside film company and will co-ordinate all the production, personnel, location and choice of director. In fact, some very famous directors started in TV advertising, notably Alan Parker (*Midnight Express*), Ridley Scott (*Bladerunner*) and Adrian Lyne (*Fatal Attraction*).

Art Directors

Art directors may begin their careers as graphic designers or artists with a good grounding in typography or layout. In the agency they will need to be able to translate a concept quickly into a visual image, and then work that up into more detail. For film they are often required to produce storyboards which look like cartoon strips: a series of boxes, each containing a sketch showing the progress of a film sequence, or animatics, which are worked up sketches on film with sound.

Copywriters

Copywriters think up slogans, voice-overs and any wording that will go into the advertisement. While copywriting is a skill that can be improved with practice and training, good copywriters have a knack for finding that clever, arresting phrase and capturing the imagination of the target audience. There is much clever psychology in good advertising copy. Copywriters must understand the audience and supply the right words in the right way. Examples of copy that have proved timeless would be 'It could be you' (the National Lottery) or 'Naughty but nice' (cream cakes).

Qualifications and Training

Qualifications are not always essential. However, most entrants are graduates. Those interested in copywriting will probably have A level English.

Below are listed the qualifications which are specifically designed for entry into the profession:

1. Copywriting/Art Direction
HND in Design Advertising, Doncaster College
HND in Advertising (Copywriting and Art Direction) Falmouth College of Arts
HND in Design (Advertising Option), Newcastle College
HND in Design (Advertising Option – includes Copywriting and Art Direction), Stockport College of Further and Higher Education
HND in Graphic Design and Advertising (with Art Direction and Copywriting Options), West Thames College
HND in Business and Finance (Advertising Specialism), the London Institute (College of Distributive Trades), Stockport College of Technology, West Hertfordshire College, University of the West of England in Bristol
Certificate in Advertising/Diploma in Advertising/Diploma in Advertising, Copywriting, West Hertfordshire College
BA (Hons) in Design and Art Direction, Manchester Metropolitan University

2. Advertising and Advertising Design
HND in Advertising, Falmouth College of Arts, the London Institute, West Herts College
HND in Advertising Design, University of Wolverhampton

BA (Hons) in Advertising and Marketing, Lancaster University,
the London Institute
BA Hons in Creative Advertising Design/ BA Hons in Advertising,
Bournemouth University

3. Other Courses
There are a number of other courses which may offer a route into
advertising: most notably, Graphic Design HNDs and Degrees
and also degrees in Communication Studies.

The advertising industry also has its own qualifications: the
CAM certificates and diploma (awarded by the Communication,
Advertising and Marketing Education Foundation). These tend
to be taken by account executives and marketing staff, but there
is no reason why such qualifications would not be useful for a
prospective art director or copywriter. The CAM diploma covers
options for creative staff. Entry requirements for the certificate
are five GCSE/SCE subjects, two of which should be at 'A' level.
Those wishing to take the diploma should have the Certificate
and a year's experience. The certificate will normally take two
years, usually at evening classes.

Personal Qualities

All advertising staff need commitment. They may need to stay
late or work weekends. They must be able to work creatively
under pressure. At the same time, they must show originality.
This requires discipline and stamina and persistence. Most im-
portantly, they must be good team players, able to get on with
people at all levels. They must be able to take forward the ideas
of others and accept criticism. Ultimately, those successful in
advertising have the willingness to produce the text/artwork that is
best for the campaign even if it is not 'great art'. Artistically, they
should have a feeling for uncomplicated messages and images.

Further Information

Advertising Association, 15 Wilton Road, London SW1 1LT; 0171
828 4831
Chartered Association of Designers, 29 Bedford Square, London
WC1B 3EG; 01628 524922
Communication, Advertising and Marketing Education Foundation

(CAM) (at Advertising Association address)

Institute of Practitioners in Advertising, 44 Belgravia Square, London SW1X 8QR; 0171 235 7020

Chapter 2

Art and Design

Art and design is a broad based term covering many different careers and occupations. There are over 100 subject titles of courses in art and design. Some courses are geared to the needs of specific industries and some may be very technical; others place an emphasis on artistic expression and creativity. This chapter begins with a simple guide to education for art and design and qualifications and training covering both young people and mature entrants. It should provide some understanding of how the education system works with regard to art and design.

Education for Art and Design

Schools cannot teach the range of art and design activities found in the outside professional world. They will, in the main, cover the core drawing, painting and craft skills. If you are considering higher education in a specialised area, you are unlikely to gain experience of the subject at school. It is therefore important to consider carefully the alternative qualifications that are on offer. There are alternative routes for mature students.

1. BTEC First Diploma or GNVQ Intermediate in Art and Design

This is a one-year general course and can be taken from year 12. Specialised subject options become available after progression on to the BTEC National or GNVQ Advanced Courses (eg Graphic Design).

Entry requirements. No formal entry requirements.

2. BTEC National Diploma or GNVQ Advanced in General Art and Design

This is a two-year course and it may be taken as an alternative to A levels by school students. Progression is on to Higher National Diplomas or degree. There are specialised National Diplomas or GNVQ Advanced Courses for specific subject areas (Fashion/3-D Design/Graphics/etc). Progression is on to Higher National Diplomas or degree.

Entry requirements: Successful completion of a BTEC First/GNVQ Intermediate or four GCSEs/SCEs at grade C or above, plus presentation of a portfolio.

3. Foundation Courses

Almost all degree courses in art and design require students to have completed a foundation course, although those with two A levels may *occasionally* be allowed *direct entry* by the college. In Scotland, foundation studies are included in full-time degree and vocational courses. Some foundation courses give a broad ground-ing in all aspects of art and design. They provide students with the opportunity to work in a variety of materials. These will include printmaking and textiles, painting and three-dimensional design. These are sometimes known as diagnostic courses. These courses will enable you to decide which branch of art and design you want to progress to (ie Visual Communication/Three Dimensional De-sign/Fashion/Specialist Areas).

Many school students keep other options open by taking A Levels prior to a foundation course.

Foundation courses are usually *very* competitive. Some local education authorities will only fund those attending locally.

Entry requirements. Minimum age 17; five GCSEs/SCEs at grade C or above; some colleges prefer at least one A level subject.

4. A Levels

While A levels provide the main and traditional route into higher education for almost all other subject areas, this is not the case with art and design courses. To gain entry with A levels is the exception. However, it is always possible where exceptional abil-ity or experience can be demonstrated. This is known as *direct entry*.

Many students do take A levels and then a foundation course. Most foundation courses will ask students coming straight from school to have at least one A level. Students pursuing this route may consider business studies as a useful additional A level to art. Success in art and design may require business acumen or entail self-employment. Many of the higher level courses have a business content.

5. City & Guilds Courses

A number of full-time City & Guilds courses are offered at colleges in the arts and crafts areas. They can range from footwear to stone masonry. Many more courses are offered part time to be studied in conjunction with employment on a day or block-release basis.

Mature Student Entry Into Higher Education

- For mature students, entry into art and design can be via the same educational route described above with particular emphasis on foundation courses. There is an additional and attractive option for mature students which is the Access course. These are one-year or two-year full- or part-time courses designed for adults returning to education. Check with your local careers service or college or Adult Education Service for details of courses in your area.
- Many local Adult Education Services offer portfolio preparation classes for those wishing to make applications for foundation courses. Contact your local education authority to check on local provision.
- The Open College of the Arts (OCA) provides courses in art and design for both interest and accreditation. The college has a network of regional programmes, providing a distance learning opportunity for students. It works in the same way as the Open University. Credits awarded by the OCA can be put toward university qualifications. For more information, contact the OCA, Houndhill, Worsbrough, Barnsley, South Yorkshire S70 6TU; 01226 730495.

Qualifications and Training

It is important for those intending to undertake a course in art and design to note that no specific level of education is indispensable for, or guarantees, any particular type or level of job. Career progression in these industries is achieved on merit, through experience, as expressed in a portfolio of work. Entry into the job market is very competitive and in almost all cases will require some relevant full-time training. To get that first job, sound course selection is essential. This is made difficult by the fact that courses with the same title and at the same level will not have the same emphasis or content. No two courses are the same. Thorough research will be required.

The picture is further confused by the fact that art and design has its own unique qualifications and educational routes. It is essential that these are understood. The situation is clarified in Table 1 below which provides a general summary of course titles: what they mean generally; and likely educational progression. Figure 1 on page 16 shows the educational routes.

Table 1 *General summary of art and design qualifications*

Type of Education	Name of Qualification	Progression
Work-based Qualifications	NVQs City & Guilds (part-time)	These qualifications are studied for while working and will normally qualify to craft level.
Further Education (Vocational)	GNVQ Intermediate GNVQ Advanced City & Guilds (full-time)	These courses are designed for entry into employment. At the GNVQ Advanced level they also qualify students for entry into higher education.
Further Education (Academic)	Foundation Courses 'A' Levels	These courses are designed as preparation for higher education. The foundation course is the preferred method of entry.

Higher Education	Higher National Diploma Degrees	HNDs and Degrees offer very specific courses. It is important to research the content carefully.
Postgraduate and Advanced Studies	Entry into Special Occupations – Art Therapy – Art Administration – Teaching – Specialist MAs/Diplomas	At postgraduate level you may wish to: 1. extend specialist art education; 2. qualify for a specialist occupation.
Professional Qualifications	CSD (Chartered Society of Designers) RAA (Royal Academy of Arts) BDS (British Display Society) ATI (Associate of the Textile Institute) LSDC (Licentiate of Society of Designer Craftsmen)	These qualifications allow you to become a member of the professional body particular to your chosen area of art and design.
Mature Students	Access Portfolio Preparation	While mature students may use the traditional routes outlined above, Access courses have been specially designed to cater for the needs of adults returning to education. Portfolio preparation courses assist those with artwork to put it in order for higher education applications.

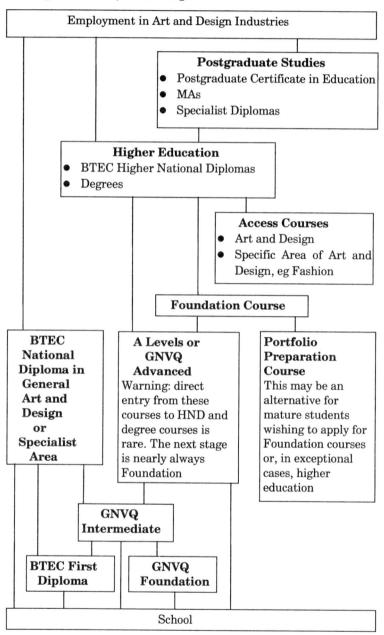

Figure 1 *Qualification routes in art and design*

What is Art and Design?

It is difficult to separate out the different areas of art and design both on paper and in practice. It is very confusing when reading reference books to understand the terminology or even find the correct course. For example, graphic design might be found under visual communication or communication design. Industrial design is also known as product design and comes under the general heading three-dimensional design. The general headings below should help.

- *Fine Art.* This includes painting and sculpture and is only a career area for those with the talent to sell original work.
- *Design.* This might be called 'applied art'. It includes:
  Visual Communication/Communication Design.
  Including: graphic design, illustration, typography and photography (see Chapter 8).
  Three-Dimensional Design. Including: industrial design, interior decorator, interior designer, furniture design (see Chapter 4), theatre design (see Chapter 12), and ceramics (see Chapter 4).
  Textiles and Fashion (see Chapter 5).
- *Allied Professions*: art therapist; arts administrator; community artist.

This chapter will cover the areas of fine art and design which are not covered by other chapters and allied professions to art.

Fine Art

Artist/Sculptor

Only a small number of artists are able to earn a living solely by the sale of original work to clients. Many more artists work as designers in advertising, industry and publishing, the latter also offering opportunities for illustrators, or teach art in school or college.

Those artists who exist solely or partly on their work have various outlets open to them. Municipal galleries run by local authorities may give exhibitions showing local artists' work with the possibility of a sale to a member of the public. There are private galleries that sell on a commission basis and subsidised galleries supported by the Arts Council or local arts associations. Artists may approach retailers who specialise in their sort of work. Artists will often sell at local markets and at festivals and fairs.

There are limited opportunities for work as a community artist (see page 31), community arts officer and artist in residence. The majority of painters and sculptors also teach. This requires undertaking art teacher training. Others combine fine art with design in areas related to their skills, in particular book illustration or advertising. A few artists may undertake picture restoration. In all these areas there are few openings.

Qualifications and Training

For the majority of artists academic qualifications are necessary. Those with aspirations toward 'pure' art may consider a degree in Fine Art. Courses include specialisms in painting, sculpture, printmaking and time-based mixed media. Fine artists learn to use many new and traditional materials, including the new technologies of computer imaging and holography.

Below are listed the higher education institutions which offer Fine Art Degrees (unless otherwise stated)

Barnsley College
Bath College of Higher Education
Blackburn College
Bolton Institute (Combined Studies)
Bretton Hall College of Higher Education
University of Brighton
Byam Shaw School of Art
Cardiff Institute of Higher Education
University of Central England
University of Central Lancashire
Central St Martins' School of Art and Design
Chelsea College of Art and Design
Cheltenham and Gloucester College of Higher Education
Cleveland College of Art and Design
Coventry University
Cumbria College of Art and Design
De Montfort University
University of Derby
University of East London

Falmouth College of Arts
Goldsmiths College
Hastings College of Art and Technology (Dip HE)
University of Hertfordshire
Kent Institute of Art and Design
Kingston University
Leeds Metropolitan University
Liverpool John Moores University
London Guildhall University
Loughborough College of Art and Design
Manchester Metropolitan University
Mid Cheshire College
Middlesex University
Mid Warwickshire College of Further Education
North Brook College Sussex
University of Northumbria
Norwich School of Art and Design
Nottingham Trent University
Oxford Brookes University
University of Plymouth
Robert Gordon University
University of Salford
Sheffield Hallam University
Solihull College
Southampton Institute
Southport College
Staffordshire University
University of Sunderland
Surrey Institute of Art & Design
University of Ulster
University of West England
Wigan and Leigh College (HND)
Winchester School of Art
Wirral Metropolitan College

Starting Salary

Designers £11–12,000 and teachers a minimum of £13,500. For
those who are self-employed there is no accurate figure.

Further Information

Regional Arts Boards will be able to help aspiring artists with contacts in their local area and advice on how best to take the local opportunities available.

Eastern Arts, Cherry Hinton Hall, Cherry Hinton Road, Cambridge CB1 4DW; 01223 215355 (Beds, Cambs, Essex, Herts, Lincs, Norfolk, Suffolk)

East Midland Arts, Mountfields House, Forest Road, Loughborough, Leics LE11 3HU; 01509 218292 (Northants, Derby, Leics, Notts)

London Arts Board, Elme House, 133 Long Acre, London WC2E 9AF; 0171 240 1313

North West Arts Board, 12 Harter Street, Manchester M16 6HY; 01612 283062 (greater Manchester, Merseyside, Derbyshire (High Peaks) Lancashire, Cheshire)

Northern Arts, 10 Osborne Terrace, Newcastle Upon Tyne NE2 1NZ; 0191 281 6334 (Tyne and Wear, Cleveland, Cumbria, Durham, Northumberland)

South East Arts Board, 10 Mount Emphraim, Tunbridge Wells, Kent TN4 8AS; 01892 515210 (Kent, Surrey and Sussex)

South West Arts, Bradninch Place, Gandy Street, Exeter. Devon EX4 2LS; 01392 218188 (Avon, Cornwall, Devon, Dorset except Bournemouth, Poole and Christchurch, Gloucestershire, Somerset)

Southern Arts, 13 Clement Street, Winchester SO23 9DQ; 01962 855099 (Berks, Bucks, Bournemouth, Poole and Christchurch, Isle of Wight, Hants, Oxon, W Sussex, Wilts)

West Midlands Arts, 82 Granville Street, Birmingham B1 2LH; 0121 6313121 (Herefordshire, Worcestershire, West Midlands, Shropshire, Staffs, Warwickshire)

Yorkshire and Humberside Arts, 21 Bond Street, Dewsbury, West Yorkshire WF13 3JP; 01924 455555 (Yorkshire, Humberside)

North Wales Arts, 10 Wellfield House, Bangor Gwynedd LL57 1ER; 01248 353248 (Clywd, Gwynedd, Montgomery district)

South East Wales Arts, 9 Victoria Street, Cwmbran. Gwent NP4 3JP. Tel: 01633 875075 (Cardiff, Gwent, Mid-Glam, South Glam, Radnor and Brecknock districts)

Artists' Newsletter (monthly). Includes job ads, bursaries, competitions, news, reviews. For visual artists. Available from AN Publications, PO Box 23, Sunderland SR1 1BR.

Visual Communication

Graphic Designer

Graphic designers convey a message or create an effect by visual means, using illustration, typography (using the right typeface or lettering for a piece of artwork), photography or computer. It is increasingly the case that the traditional skills can be replicated using desktop publishing packages altering word and layout on a computer screen. Manual skills are still used in the early sketching stages, and artistic training and instinct are still the cornerstone of the work. Graphic designers generally work on two-dimensional designs, creating ideas for book covers, record sleeves and captions for television. However, graphic design also incorporates three dimensional design in the forms of product packaging, exhibitions and displays.

Many graphic designers are employed by *advertising agencies* (see Chapter 1) and work alongside copywriters to design posters, newspaper and magazine advertisements and the layout for free publicity and mailshots.

Another source of employment is *design consultancies*. These are independent firms of designers employing several different kinds of designer (graphic, package, product, display, exhibition, textile, furniture, interior). They may undertake major and minor design jobs for industrial and commercial companies. For example, a new, prestige bookshop is opening shortly. The owner brings in the design consultancy to design the shop interior, all point of display fittings and all business stationery to be used – from sale wrapping paper to company invoices and sales slips. When the shop is due to open, the design team works on the promotion and publicity material and press advertisements. Some design studios may be more specific in their approach offering, for example, purely graphic design and publicity services.

Graphic designers may also work in *publishing houses* or for *magazines*. They will work as art directors or art assistants. The art director is responsible for the overall visual appearance of the publication which is decided in consultation with the editorial staff. This involves choosing the appropriate typeface, deciding on the layout of pages or book covers, and the overall design. They will often employ freelance illustrators and photographers for the necessary visual extras.

Graphic designers in *technical design* prepare plans and drawings from written specifications for the use of scientists, engineers or architects. This work involves greater accuracy and less creativity. The developments in the areas of computer illustration and computer-enhanced illustration are revolutionising this area of work. (See **Industrial Design** on page 26).

The demand for graphic designers in *television* has grown as the new technology increased the opportunity for creative art input. The work of a graphics department in television is wide ranging. It includes typography, lettering, simple credits and captions, designing mobiles, weather charts, cartoons and animation, and making props (eg 'ration books'). Graphic designers often regard themselves as experts in producing authentic copies as well as original designs. All designers are college trained with degrees or diplomas in graphic design. Most illustration work is carried out by freelance illustrators. Increasingly, the computer is used in television graphics. The application of modern technology and the multimedia will require designers to keep up with the development of this medium. Art and design college-leavers are recruited to TV as assistant designers.

After a few years' experience, graphic designers may set up on a *freelance* basis once they have the commercial experience and contacts to understand the needs of the 'niche' or market they are looking to enter. (For Further information, see Chapter 6 in *Careers in Art and Design* from Kogan Page.)

Qualifications and Training

The sections **Education for Art and Design** (page 11) and **Qualifications and Training** (page 13) cover the routes to being a graphic designer. Normally, a qualified designer would have completed either a relevant HND or Degree course. There are 80 courses in the United Kingdom which designate themselves as Graphic Design and a further 21 which describe themselves as Communication Design. (Lists of these can be found in the *Guide to Courses and Careers in Art, Craft and Design* published by National Society for Education in Art and Design (NSEAD)).

Salary

Salaries vary according to ability and the employer. A salaried designer could expect a starting salary of £10,700 to £12,000. Those with experience average £20,000.

Further Information

British Display Society, 70a Crayford High street, Dartford, Kent
DA1 4EF; 01322 550 544
The Chartered Society of Designers, 29 Bedford Square, London
WC1B 3EG; 0171 631 1510
The Design Council, 1 Oxendon Street, London SW1Y 4EE; 0171
208 2121
The Design Council (Scotland), Ca d'Oro Building, 45 Gordon
Street, Glasgow G1 3LZ
The Design Council (Wales), QED Centre, Main Avenue,
Treforest Estate, Treforest, Pontypridd CF37 5TR
Royal Academy of Arts, Burlington House, Piccadilly, London
W1V 0DS; 0171 434 0837
Society of Designer Craftsmen, 24 Rivington Street, London W1R
1LH; 0171 739 3663
Textile Institute, 10 Blackfriars Street, Manchester M3 5DR;
0161 834 845

Campaign (weekly; advertising graphic design and posts in
design consultancies)
Design Week (design appointments)

Illustrator

Illustrators combine elements of fine art and graphic design in their work, producing drawings and paintings for illustrations to accompany text in books, magazines and posters. They may also be given work by design consultancies and advertising agencies on a freelance basis. In addition, scientific and technical illustrators may find freelance work in industry, medical and scientific publishing houses, research establishments, government departments, the National Health Service and in museums. Medical illustration is regarded as a specific profession and is covered in detail in Chapter 8.

Illustration is usually done on a freelance basis but it can be difficult to get started. The Association of Illustrators provides practical help and advice on how to become freelance. Often illustrators will take other work while building up contacts. The degree show at the end of a degree or diploma may bring art directors from advertising agencies and publishing houses and advertising agents looking for new talent. Many illustrators find their first commissions this way. A direct approach to potential employers with a well presented and prepared portfolio may also bring work.

Some illustrators find it easier to work in groups and collectively rent a studio. In this way, the sense of isolation and lean times may be overcome as well as increasing the number of contacts from which the group as a whole may benefit. Some illustrators use an artists' agent who will try to find them work for a commission of 25 per cent or more.

Qualifications and Training

This is described under **Graphic Design** (page 22). There are, however, specialist higher education courses at:

(Degree unless stated)

Anglia Polytechnic University
University of Brighton
Carmarthenshire College of Technology and Art (HND)
University of Central England
University of Central Lancashire
Cleveland College of Art and Technology (HND)
Duncan Jordonstone College
Falmouth College of Arts
Gemeni School of Illustration
Herefordshire College of Art and Design (HND)
Kent Institute of Art and Design (HND)
Kingston University
Leicester South Fields College (HND)
Loughborough College of Art and Design
Middlesex University
North Brook College – Sussex (HND)
North Wales Institute of Higher Education (HND)
University of Plymouth
University of Portsmouth
St Helens College (HND)

Stockport College of Further and Higher Education (HND)
University of Sunderland (HND)
Swansea Institute of Higher Education (HND)
Swindon College (+ HND)
University of the West of England
University of Westminster
Wigan and Leigh College (HND)
University of Wolverhampton

There are also specialised technical/scientific/history illustration courses at:

Blackpool and Fylde College
Bournemouth and Poole College of Art and Design (+ HND)
Middlesex University
University of Sunderland
Swansea Institute of Higher Education

There are two other courses:

BA Illustration with Animation at Manchester Metropolitan University
HND Illustration and Media Design at Edinburgh's Telford College

Salary

This may vary according to commissions. A successful illustrator's salary will be on a par with a graphic designer.

Further Information

The Association of Illustrators, 29 Bedford Square, London EC1N 8FH; 0171 636 4100

Three-dimensional Design

Three-dimensional design as a term covers the following areas:

Industrial or Product Design

This is the aesthetic design of products whose mechanical, electrical or electronic function has already been worked out by a design engineer. The product may be a car or a piece of office furniture.

The job of the industrial or product designer is to ensure that not only is the product efficient, convenient and safe, but looks good. The designer may work closely with engineers and production staff. Any small change in a design can mean changes in tooling up for production. With strict budgets to work to, the designer must consider the implications of the design work. Some industrial design courses may include the study and application of engineering principals; others devote more time to creative elements.

Qualifications

There are 44 designated courses in Industrial or Product Design in the UK. There is also a specialised course in Transport Design at Coventry University. The educational routes are the same as those described in **Qualifications and Training** on page 13.

Interior Design

Interior designers are concerned with the organisation of space and the decoration of the interiors of: buildings, shops, hotels, office blocks, ships and aircraft, and private houses. Interior designers may join design practices – working with other designers and architects. Some may work for design practices and consultancies, offering a wide range of other services. Some may set up in private practice. Interior designers may also join office furniture and design services, or work with in-house design groups, for example with furniture manufacturers in the retail industry, providing bathroom and kitchen planning services to customers in a large department store, or with local hotel groups, building companies, and in some industrial companies.

Most interior design work is for industry, shop interiors and displays, exhibitions, office interiors, hotels, airports and public buildings. Some interior designers may apply their skills to other fields such as theatre design (see Chapter 12) or product design. They may also organise exhibitions and conferences where the 'look' needs to be right. There are many common course components with architecture courses and retail display and exhibition design. In fact, Theatre/Set Design and Exhibition and Display Design are offered as specialisms on HND and Degree courses.

Salary

This starts at around £11,000.

Qualifications and Training

The Education for Art and Design route described on page 11 applies. At HND/Degree level there are courses in Interior Architectural Design, Interior Design and Spatial Design. Check the UCAS Handbook under these headings.

Further Information

Interior Designers' and Decorators' Association, Chelsea Harbour Design Centre, Lots Road, London SW10 0XE; 0171 349 0800

Allied Professions to Art

Art Therapy

Art therapy is a relatively new profession and is allied to other remedial therapies: occupational, music and drama therapy. Art therapy has a role to play as a healing aid in improving the condition and often the quality of life for hospital patients or people with terminal or long-term illnesses, those in psychiatric care, the mentally and physically disabled and those receiving remedial tuition in schools.

Art therapy may be used as an interpretational aid. For example, psychiatric patients may find it easier to express feelings and emotions visually through painting or working with clay or wood rather than verbally. Art therapists work alongside psychiatrists and psychotherapists and encourage patients to express themselves. As well as being good teachers and facilitators, art therapists must also have an understanding of psychopathology, which is studied as part of art therapy training. In addition to finding employment in hospitals, art therapists work in special schools for the mentally and physically disabled as art teachers. Here they use art as a means of communication, in assessment, and as a way of encouraging creativity. They may also be employed by social services in day centres for those with special needs. As most posts are part time, full time therapists usually work for more than one institution in a locality.

Qualifications and Training

Most entrants to art therapy are graduates, usually in art and design subjects, and occasionally in other subjects such as education, sociology or psychology where there is evidence of artistic ability. To qualify as an art therapist requires the combination of an appropriate graduate qualification and relevant work experience.

There are a number of ways in which experience can be gained. Some people may do voluntary work in hospitals or day centres while still at college. Nursing experience is also a useful way of gaining an insight into the work and working environment. Another route into art therapy is after teacher training and a period of teaching experience in arts subjects in schools. Those teachers who are interested in remedial or specialist work may wish to pursue an art therapy course. It is also possible to combine a Postgraduate Certificate in Education (PGCE – Teacher Training) with art therapy at:

The University of Central England in Birmingham
University of Hertfordshire
University of London (Goldsmiths College)

The main qualification is the Postgraduate Diploma in Art Therapy. Entrants will usually have a degree in a relevant subject or a professional qualification in social work, occupational therapy, teaching or psychiatric nursing. One-year full-time courses are offered at:

University of Hertfordshire
University of London (Goldsmiths College)
Sheffield Hallam University

These institutions also offer a two-year part-time course for people already employed within the social services, health services or as teachers in special education.

Salary

Salaries vary greatly according to the place of employment. Therapists employed by the National Health Service earn approximately £13,900–£20,000.

Further Information

The British Association of Art Therapists, 11a Richmond Road, Brighton, East Sussex BN2 3RL (an information folder costs £5; send SAE)

Arts Administration

Arts administrators are professionals involved in the publicity, promotion and organisation of artistic events of all kinds. Arts administrators are often involved in obtaining money in addition to that received from profits made to enable the activity to continue. To do this they may need to contact representatives from local councils, politicians and private companies for funding. Currently, arts administrators may be expected to receive or prepare bids for National Lottery monies where their projects are community based.

Likely places of employment are listed below:

The Arts Council. Its chief role is to administer government aid to the arts. There are relatively few jobs at their headquarters. The Officers in Literature, Music, Drama and Visual Arts have experience and qualifications in their own specialised fields. There are a few assistant administrative and secretarial posts for which competition is fierce.

The Crafts Council performs a similar function to the Arts Council, but is devoted to the promotion and financing of crafts such as jewellery, ceramics, glass, weaving and so on.

Regional Arts Boards perform the same function at a regional level, administering funding for the Arts and the Crafts Council, organising publicity for the arts, liaising with local authorities, supporting and promoting young artists, performers and crafts-people in the area. There are posts such as drama officers, crafts officers, community arts officers. These involve committee work, receiving grant applications, liaising with local societies, art groups and sometimes colleges. There may also be public relations and publicity posts.

Arts centres, theatres, ballet, opera, concert halls. Posts exist in stage management, publicity, front of house management, and so on. As well as managing and organising programmes of events, administrators meet the needs of resident and visiting companies, and there is often the general maintenance and care of the building to consider. The job also involves the management of the general office and provision of catering and the maintaining of licensed premises. Community theatre groups, touring companies and orchestras may also employ arts administrators.

Community arts is mentioned on page 31. There is a role for those with administrative skills to work in this field.

Art and craft galleries and shops. Opportunities may exist in national and provincial galleries for exhibition organisers and publicity officers, and administrators in private galleries. Some galleries at universities employ full-time or part-time exhibition staff.

Arts festivals. Many cities and towns throughout the country have annual festivals of arts events, performances and exhibitions. Some of the larger festivals employ full- or part-time staff as organisers. The Arts Council publishes a list of festivals and their dates each year.

Local authorities run museums and art galleries, leisure and amenity centres, conference centres, recreation and sports complexes where there may be opportunities for a career in municipal entertainment, recreation and leisure management. In addition, some local authorities employ arts officers who liaise with the Regional Arts Boards and arts societies in the area.

Private galleries. There are many private galleries in most major cities, dealing with a portfolio of artists for whom they sell and organise exhibitions. The most famous are in London in the areas covered by Cork Street, New Bond Street and Burlington Arcade.

Qualifications and Training

Experience is often more important than formal educational requirements although a good general education is expected. There are two full time courses in Arts Administration which run in conjunction with the Arts Council at the City University's Centre for the Arts. Both are post-experience or postgraduate courses. There are a small number of first degree courses which offer HND and first degree courses in Arts Administration. These are:

HND Arts and Events Administration, Bournemouth and Poole College of Art and Design

BA Performing Arts (Arts Administration Option), De Montfort
   University
BA Art for Society, University of Wolverhampton
BA Art in a Community Context, University of West London
   (Roehampton Institute)
Postgraduate Diploma in Arts Management, University of
   Northumbria at Newcastle
MA Arts Administration, MA in Museum and Gallery
   Management, City University
MSC/MBA Arts Management (Part of Business Studies), Durham
   University

Those wishing to take the examinations of the Institute of Chartered Secretaries and Administrators can enter at three levels.
To enter at the first level (the Foundation Programme) there are no
specific entry requirements. The level must be completed before
going on to the Pre-professional programme and the Professional
Programme. Graduates or equivalent do have some exemptions.

Salary

This starts at around £11,000 as an assistant

Further Information

The Arts Council, 14 Great Peter Street, London SW1 3NQ; 0171
   333 0100
Arts Council of Northern Ireland, 181 Stramillas Road, Belfast
   BT9 5DU; 01232 381591
Arts Council of Wales, Holst House, Museum Place, Cardiff CF1
   3NX; 01222 394711
The Crafts Council, 44a Pentonville Road, London N1 9BY; 0171
   278 7700
Institute of Chartered Secretaries and Administrators, 16 Park
   Crescent, London W1N 4AH; 0171 580 4741
Scottish Arts Council, 12 Manor Place, Edinburgh EH3 7DD;
   0131 2266051

Community Artist

For years, many artists and performers have taken active roles
in their own communities and encouraged other people to express
themselves through artistic means – by teaching, community

work, adult education classes and so on. In recent years, some of the artists and performers have established a new identity, calling themselves community artists.

At the start, most community artists were unpaid. They worked with local groups in a variety of ways: setting up a community newspaper; helping residents create their own play or music; working on creative projects with play schemes. The artist became a facilitator, an organiser, a teacher of skills to people who wished to express themselves and their ideas through participating in theatre, music, dance, the visual arts, video, film, radio, crafts, photography and puppetry.

The number of community arts projects has grown from 100 in the 1980s to 1,000 currently. Many of these receive funding from Regional Arts Boards or direct from the Community Arts Panel of the Arts Council of Great Britain, from local authorities or charities, though with present expenditure cuts the future of many projects may be uncertain. Here are some examples of the places where community artists may work:

- A *community arts centre* with its own premises for play activities for local children may have been set up by volunteers. Once established, permanent and salaried posts may be created. Workers and volunteers may help run community festivals; arts/crafts classes; theatre groups; dance; provide printing facilities for local clubs or pressure groups to print their own posters.
- *Summer play schemes; adventure playgrounds.*
- Some *local authorities* and new *town development corporations* employ community artists for community development work: helping bring residents together; running leisure activities; teaching arts and crafts skills.
- Some town artists work with *planners and architects* in planning the living environments in new towns.
- *Regional Arts Boards* may employ community arts workers in conjunction with the local authority to initiate projects in a given area.

Community artists have some kind of creative skill to contribute and many are all-round artists who have had art or drama school training. As a relatively new profession, little formal training exists, although there are some art and design and performance courses with a social community element. There are no rigid career structures or entry requirements. Few full-time salaried posts exist. On the whole, community artists find it difficult to see their work as a long term career. Hours are irregular, badly paid or on a voluntary basis, and there is little job security.

Trained teachers, art therapists, fine artists, actors, photographers, dancers and drama students in other employment regularly make a contribution to community arts activities.

Those who wish to make this a full-term career must be dedicated and have high ideals about the importance of their work.

Qualifications and Training

While this is still a growing profession, there is little specific training available. A proficiency in the general arts subjects is required. However, as the profession picks up momentum, some degree course titles have emerged which would be relevant to the job. These include:

BA Art Practice and the Community, Roehampton Institute
BA Community Arts, City College Manchester

Some degrees in Performance Arts may also contain relevant options.

Salary

This can vary from nothing to very low.

Further Information

New Statesman (weekly)
Time Out (weekly)

See also **Artist/Sculptor** (page 17).

Chapter 3

Broadcasting

Television and radio in the UK run as a public service and on a commercial basis, providing information, education and entertainment. The British Broadcasting Corporation (BBC) financed largely by a licence fee has two television channels and 43 local radio stations. Independent television and radio stations regulated by the Independent Broadcasting Authority are financed by advertising. There are 15 independent regional companies, Channel Four and Sianel Pedwar Cymru (S4C) its Welsh Counterpart, GMTV and Independent Television News (ITN) and 120 local independent radio stations. In 1997, Channel 5 will be launched. Add to this Satellite Broadcasting, which currently operates ten themed channels, and cable broadcasting and you have a major employment market. It is notoriously difficult to get started in radio and television. Anybody can say they want to work in this area – the problem is that there are thousands of people with the same vague media ambitions. It is important that you are clearly focused on what you want to do and on the possible routes of entry.

Qualifications and Training

There are hundreds of media-related courses with more appearing each year. However, the broadcasting organisations, although appreciating the standard of courses, do not recognise them officially. It is therefore important that you research your courses thoroughly. Speak to the recruitment managers at the kinds of organisation you hope to work for – take their recommendations. Check with the course tutors on the destinations of their graduates or diplomates.

Higher Education
A number of institutions offer higher education HND and Degree courses which may be relevant to the broadcasting industry in getting into the technical production and creative film-making part of broadcasting. These are:

Film and Television Production
Bournemouth and Poole College of Art and Design, Cleveland College of Art and Design, North East Wales Institute of Higher Education, St Helens College.

Film and Video
University of Derby, Gwent College of Higher Education, Surrey Institute of Higher Education.

Interactive and Broadcast Media
Gwent College of Higher Education, Manchester Metropolitan University.

Media Production
Cheltenham & Gloucester College of Higher Education, Cumbria College of Higher Education, Dewsbury College of Higher Education, University of Humberside, University of Northumbria, Plymouth College of Art and Design, University of Portsmouth, St Helens College, Staffordshire University; Stoke on Trent College, West Herts College, University of Westminster, North East Worcester College.

Photography, Television and Film
Salisbury College

Television Operations
Northumberland College, Ravensbourne College of Design and Communication

Television Production Design
Nottingham Trent University

Video Production
James Watt College of Further and Higher Education

Entry Level Courses and Training Schemes

Association of Independent Radio Companies (AIRC)
The AIRC maintains an extensive database of current training courses in radio. For further information, contact AIRC, 46 Westbourne Grove, London WC2 5SH; 0171 727 2646.

Film and Television Freelance Training (FT2)
FT2 offers an introduction to some of the technical and production jobs in radio and television. Its New Entrants Technical Training Scheme is a full-time two-year course which trains entrants to become freelance technical assistants in specific areas including editing, sound and hair and make-up. The style is that of an apprenticeship with 80 per cent of the time spent on attachments with film and television crews. This is supplemented by general and specific periods of training in theory and practical work.

Applicants to FT2 must be over 18 and registered as being unemployed. In most cases the requirements are demonstrable talent, commitment and determination. However, the competition for places is fierce with 150 applications per place. For further information, write to FT2, Fourth Floor, Dean Street, London W1V 5RN; 0171 734 5141.

Community Service Volunteers (CSV) Media
CSV Media is the largest media training agency in the UK. It works in partnership with over 100 local TV and radio stations and offers nationally validated training in a range of media skills. CSV trains unemployed young people and adults at over 40 sites nationwide, concentrating on practical, on-the-job experience. Contact CSV Media, 237 Pentonville Road, London N1 9NJ; 0171 278 6601.

National Film and Television School (See Chapter 6, page 67)

London International Film School (See Chapter 6, page 68)

Skillset
Skillset is the industry training organisation for the broadcast, film and video sectors. Founded in 1992 and recognised by the Department for Education and Employment, it provides relevant

training information. Currently, it is setting up a database with the British Film Institute and local Regional Arts Boards of long and short courses available. For further information, send an SAE to Skillset, 124 Horseferry Road, London SW1P 2TX; 0171 306 8585.

Jobs in Broadcasting

This chapter will give a brief summary of jobs in the broadcast media. As this book is covering a large subject area there is not the space to cover all the jobs that the broadcast industry encompasses, many of which are non-creative. Those which are covered are potentially entrant jobs which are, in some sense, creative. The jobs are listed in alphabetical order.

Camera Operator

Two kinds of camera are used in television: electronic (or video) cameras which record on a magnetic strip and are used for live transmissions; and film cameras, which are mainly used for commercials and feature-length dramas.

Camera operators are usually recruited at the age of 18+ and trained on the job. Applicants should have a good general education, GCSEs/SCEs in English, maths and preferably a science, and possess some knowledge of optics, film and television photography.

The work of a camera operator is tiring, involving hours of standing under hot studio lights. The hours are often anti-social and camera crews can be required to work away from base, often in uncomfortable conditions for long periods.

Electronic Camera Operator
In a studio there may be up to six electronic (video) cameras, each operated by one person assisted by camera crew members. Most of these cameras will be pedestal mounted, but some may be on a jib. Camera operators may work standing or sitting behind a pedestal-operated camera, or they may have to sit at the end of a camera jib. An outside broadcast unit will work from a small remote control room. Operators may find themselves working on a roof top or scaffolding tower. Heights must not be a fear.

Experienced operators may decide the framing and composition of the picture, but will be guided by the director on how the action must be shot. They must be able to service the equipment themselves, edit tapes and use electronic links communication. Some companies start their trainees operating cameras early on, but others make them spend several months operating cranes and laying cables. It usually takes six years to become fully trained, and promotion to the top grades takes 10 to 20 years.

Film Camera Operator/Lighting Camera Operator

Trainees begin by performing such tasks as pulling focus, loading and charging magazines, checking and cleaning equipment. Senior film operators – also known as lighting camera operators – are responsible for the technical and artistic quality of the pictures and, with the director, share major decisions about camera positioning, lighting and how the action should be shot.

Training. A number of traineeships are offered by employers (BBC/ITV companies). The competition is fierce. They are now training multi-skilled technicians over a range of equipment (camera operator/camera sound/editing techniques). FT2 (see page 36) offers 20 places for technicians. Cyfle has six places each year to train Welsh-speaking technicians; The Gaelic Television Training Trust has eight grants each year for Gaelic speakers; Channel Four finances two training schemes a year for people with disabilities or from ethnic backgrounds. It is also possible to train in higher education (see **Qualifications and Training** on page 34).

Costume Designer

Costume designers work in the area of television light entertainment and drama. They begin by reading the programme script then, in liaison with the producer, director, choreographer and set designer, plan the costumes and work out the costume budget. Costume designers should have a good grounding in the history of costume and etiquette and be creative and innovative, while possessing administrative and supervisory skills. Some television companies have their own stocks of costumes while others rely on costumiers. Costume design assistant vacancies are one of the entry points into this profession. The assistant's job includes arranging fittings and researching and shopping for fabrics.

Training. There are Degree Courses in Costume for the Screen/Performance Arts at Bournemouth and Poole College of

Art and Design and the London College of Fashion (part of the London Institute); and in Costume Design and Wardrobe at the Rose Bruford College. HND and Degree Courses in Theatre Design may also offer costume as an option.

Editor – Film, Videotape, Electronic News Gathering

The editor works closely with the producer and director preparing the final version of a programme. The work demands great attention to detail, precision and creativity and the skills take a long time to assimilate. Ironically, the better the editor the less conscious the viewer will be of his or her work.

Film Editor
Film, unlike videotape, is cut and spliced. The film editor studies each frame and decides which to remove and where to insert shots. Increasingly, editors are becoming multiskilled and learning to work on all formats. The assistant film editor, who does not make editing decisions, helps the editor by logging film in and out, doing joins, synchronising rushes and keeping in touch with film processing laboratories.

Videotape Editor
Most television programmes are recorded on videotape cassettes. When edit points have been decided, the sections of tape are recorded on to another tape. Editing machines are complicated pieces of equipment but relatively easy to learn the operate. It is not necessary to have a technical background to become a videotape editor, although many start out as television engineers or technicians. The assistant videotape editor does support work for the editor, such as keeping records and lining up the machines for use.

Electronic News Gathering Editor
ENG editors use the same techniques as videotape editors. They have to meet deadlines for news bulletins and work under great pressure. ENG operators are expected to be able to maintain and repair their own equipment, as many of them work away from base.

Training. See FT2 on page 36. Also the BBC and ITV companies recruit for multiskilled technicians to fill their needs.

Floor Manager

Floor managers have an important and demanding job. They co-ordinate everything that happens on the studio floor, from checking that props are in place to making sure that performers know where to stand and what to do. They also give cues and prompts and, when there is a studio audience, the floor manager takes charge of that too. During studio recordings and rehearsals, the programme director watches proceedings on monitors and passes on instructions to the floor manager on headphones.

Floor managers usually start their careers as assistants and need to be thoroughly familiar with every aspect of television production. Essential qualities are stamina, tact, organising ability and great calm. Trainees should have a good general education and experience of working in theatre.

Training. Again, the FT2 training scheme (page 36) may provide a point of entry. Also courses which include stage management may be useful for entry. The training for camera operator or sound technician may also be useful when applying for jobs.

Graphic Designer

The graphic designer is responsible for designing and supervising the execution of all graphic programme material, including credits, charts, graphs, logos and even some props, such as documents used in drama. The graphic designer must be highly creative but also capable of adapting concepts to suit the production staff and must work closely with the programme's producer, director, set designer and sometimes, when developing a title sequence, the composer of the title music. A graphic design department can also employ photographers and photographic assistants.

Training. See Chapter 2, **Graphic Designer**, pages 21–2.

Journalism and Newswork

Journalism is a very important part of any broadcasting organisation's output. An assortment of people are involved in news gathering, writing and presentations, but everyone from the news typist to the foreign correspondent works under intense pressure. There are strict deadlines, bulletins are always broadcast live and stories must constantly be updated. Newswork never stops and with early morning and late night news bulletins, it involves unsociable hours, weekend duties and night shifts.

Stories come from various sources, including news agencies, stringers (freelance news correspondents), the police and newspaper reporters.

The news editor decides on the content of the bulletin and the weighting of the items that make it up. He or she decides which items to follow up and sends a reporter to cover each story. The major news organisations, such as ITN and the BBC, also employ specialist correspondents who have expert knowledge in a particular field to provide in-depth coverage.

Journalists

There is fierce competition for journalists' posts in broadcasting. Applicants for traineeships generally hold a good degree or equivalent, and all can show good examples of their work in newspaper articles or on audio or videotape. Often recruits are taken from the print or radio media. The BBC also advertise for traineeships for local radio when there is a need to recruit new staff.

News Readers

These are likely to be drawn from trained journalists already working within the broadcasting industry.

Training. There are many ways of training for a career in journalism. These include Degree courses at Bournemouth University, University of Central Lancashire, City University, the London Institute, (London College of Printing (LCP)), Nottingham Trent University, University of Wales, and West Surrey College of Art and Design. Some college and school-leavers and some graduates are recruited by training schemes operated by the National Council for the Training of Journalists (NCTJ) linked to local newspaper recruitment. There is also the National Council for the Training of Broadcast Journalists (NCTBJ) which works with the BBC, the National Union of Journalists and the Association of Independent Radio Companies (see page 36) to produce guidelines to approve courses. Details of NCTBJ courses can be obtained by sending an SAE to the NCTBJ, 188 Lichfield Court, Sheen Road, Richmond, Surrey TW9 1BB; 0181 940 0694.

Lighting Director

Lighting directors decide how to position lights in order to get the best effect on a given set. In a chat show, for example, this would be comparatively straightforward, but in drama lighting is used to create atmosphere and illusion. Lighting directors prepare plans for and supervise the work of lighting electricians and lighting console operators. They must liaise with the programme director, the set designer and other members of the production team, such as make-up artists. Lighting directors require both flair and technical ability. They are usually recruited internally.

Make-up Artist

Make-up artists spend much of their time doing corrective work, such as combing hair and powdering noses. The creative aspect of the job comes to the fore in drama and light entertainment for which they may be required to do elaborate face and body make-up, style hair and wigs or produce effects such as scars or bruises.

Make-up artists need a calm, tactful personality as they work with many different sorts of people – actors, politicians, ordinary members of the public – all of whom are likely to be nervous before going on camera.

Training. Qualifications sought are A level standard (preferred subjects: art, history, English) plus beauty therapy/hairdressing/art school training. The minimum age for traineeships is 20-21. Experience in make-up in amateur theatre is very useful.

Producer

Producers turn ideas into programmes. They head the production team and are responsible for managing the programme budget and scheduling rehearsals. They also have a say in the selection of programme participants. In radio, the producer often initiates and researches the initial idea and records the material, although these duties can be shared with a researcher and a production assistant. In television, it is the producer who will have conceived or contributed to the idea on which the programme is based. In some cases the producer will also direct.

Producers must be receptive to the ideas of others and be able to originate suitable programme concepts. They also need to understand the requirements of the network or region they work in. It may be possible to specialise in the producing of particular types of programme: music, sport or current affairs, for example. As the TV and radio stations are increasingly contracting out their programmes, the job title Independent Producer has been created. This usually refers to a person who runs an independent production company seeking commissions from the regional networks and developing ideas. These are usually very small – employing only when they successfully commission.

Training. Most vacancies are filled by internal applicants who have worked their way up through researcher and production assistant. There are a few traineeships for the posts in television and radio.

Production Assistant

Production assistants work on a particular programme from start to finish, providing support services for the producer and the director. They attend all the programme planning meetings, take notes of the decisions made and see that the required action is taken. This may mean retyping the script after a rehearsal run through. Many production assistants do the work of the continuity person. In the final run-through of a TV programme, the production assistant sits with the director in the control room and instructs the camera operators over the talkback system. In both radio and television the production assistant times the recordings with a stopwatch. He or she also provides any information needed by those in post-production work, such as editing.

Production assistants also work on live programmes, for example news broadcasts where the atmosphere in the control room can be very tense. The job requires excellent organisational skills, attention to detail, calm, initiative and the ability to manage and get on with all types of people.

Training. A lot of PAs are recruited as trainees, and many vacancies are filled by people already in broadcasting. Many applicants are graduates with secretarial/administrative experience. Esther Rantzen started on a secretarial course with the BBC and came through to be a production assistant and researcher.

Programme Director

In television, the programme director is in charge of the shooting of the programme and the direction of performers and crew. TV drama productions involve detailed shot-by-shot work. The director places the actors and discusses their interpretation of the roles and, after consultation with the technical experts, decides on lighting effects and camera angles. When shooting is completed, the director supervises post-production work, such as editing and sound dubbing. In radio drama, the director rehearses the actors, selects sound effects, and again supervises post-production. In live broadcasts, such as news bulletins, the programme director follows a running order, selects pictures and relays instructions to the presenters.

Training. Most vacancies are filled by internal applicants with substantial production experience.

Researcher

Behind every successful programme there will have been a hard-working, competent researcher. The exact job description will vary from programme to programme, but duties can include lining up and interviewing contacts, conducting vox pops, finding locations, digging through statistical information, checking through archives and scriptwriting. Researchers are also expected to contribute ideas to the programme. They can specialise: some companies employ researchers specifically to find suitable contestants for their quiz and game shows.

Training. Most researchers have either gained experience in research as a journalist or editorial assistant on a newspaper or magazine or as a production assistant. However, FT2 does have the research function as part of its two year New Entrants Training Scheme (see page 36).

Script Editor

Script editors work in drama departments in close consultation with programme producers. Their duties can include commissioning writers, finding new writing talent, conducting research and rewriting material. In the case of a long running serial, where a number of writers are needed to contribute different episodes, sometimes over a period of years, the script editor ensures that each is written in a uniform style and that plot and character details remain consistent. The script editor may also be responsible for developing storylines.

Essential qualities for the job are tact, patience, an excellent memory and a genuine love of reading and drama.

Training. Script editors generally have a literary background and have worked in theatre, reading and reporting on unsolicited scripts.

Set Designer

Every television programme, from a panel game to a drama, has been designed to create a certain ambience. Designers work with producers and directors and must understand the technical processes of production and have a feeling for how the content of the programme should be visually interpreted. The work requires a knowledge of the history of art and architecture. Many studio sets are viewed in close up and from many different angles, so a great deal of planning goes into them. Designers have to take into account the positioning and movement of performers, props, cameras cables, microphone booms and lighting. They normally construct a scale model of a set for use in programme meetings and produce simplified architectural drawings. When a set design has been agreed, plans are sent to the workshop and construction begins. Scenic artists work under the set designer and paint the sets, often creating effects (for example, a marble floor). Their job is highly skilled and requires a thorough knowledge of styles in architecture, painting and furniture.

Training. Set designers almost always begin as assistant designers having obtained a degree in Interior Design, Art and Design, Stage Design or Architecture. Scenic arists will usually have a degree in Fine Art (see Chapter 2, page 17).

Sound Operator

Sound operators are employed in film, radio and television and their work requires both creative and technical skills. In radio, the sound operator is usually also the studio manager. Duties might include: setting up the studio for shoots, operating tape recorders, sound balancing and mixing, and editing audio tapes. The sound operator works under instructions from the producer/director. In television, they ensure that the studio equipment is functioning properly and, working with the camera operators, they see that microphone booms are effectively positioned and yet remain out of shot. Sound operators will also do a lot of pre- and post-production work, such as editing taped speech and music or selecting special sound effects. On outside broadcasts, sound operators will be responsible for rigging up and dismantling equipment and for testing the quality of the lines.

Training. This is the same as for camera operator (ie general technician training – see pages 37–8). Drama school stage management courses include Theatre Lighting and Sound. City of Westminster College offers a one year course in Lighting and Sound which was evolved with the Association of British Theatre Technicians.

Transmission Controller

Transmission controllers are responsible for sending the company's programmes to the transmitters so that they are broadcast at the advertised times. They work from a mixer console connected to a bank of television screens on which they can monitor the picture that is currently being sent from the station to the transmitter, the picture going from the transmitter to home TV screens, and the start of the next programme to be broadcast. The transmission controller operates the controls to ensure that each programme is brought in on cue. The work involves a great deal of planning and combines periods of intense activity with periods when nothing happens. Controllers need to be able to think and act quickly in the event of a failure as they must not leave the viewer with a blank screen.

Training. Applicants for assistant transmission controller vacancies are usually aged between 18 and 21. They need normal colour vision, good hearing and will usually have A levels or a degree.

Vision Mixer

Television programmes are generally made up from pictures that come from a number of different sources, such as a camera in a studio, or maybe a pre-recorded videotape or from a slide. Vision mixers receive a signal from the director telling them when to cut from one picture to another, producing a smooth sequence of images. The vision mixer sits at a console to which all the picture sources are fed. This console can produce special effects, such as dissolving or wiping, to make the transition from one scene to another more unobtrusive or interesting. The job calls for quick reactions and a good sense of timing.

Training. Trainees are usually recruited from among those already working in television production.

Visual Effects Designer

Many of those concerned with the visual side of television – set designers, costume designers, make-up artists – are creating a visual effect or illusion. The services of visual effects designers are called upon when the illusion required is on a grander scale, such as a burning skyscraper or rocket launch. They may work with actors or stunt performers (using a controlled fire) on a life-size set or they may use scale models (to blow up a building). Visual effects designers need a good working knowledge of sculpture, model making, painting, optics and pyrotechnics, together with an understanding of the principles of physics, chemistry and electricity. Many other visual effects are generated electronically. There are few permanent posts in television. Most work freelance for facility houses which provide services for film and television companies.

Training. Usually an art college HND or Degree or an electronics qualification. Vacancies in this field are very rare.

Further Information

Association of British Theatre Technicians, 47 Bermondsey St, London SE1 3XF; 0171 403 3778

BBC Corporate Recruitment Services, White City, Wood Lane, London W12 7TS; 0171 752 5252

British Sky Broadcasting, 6 Centaurs Business Park, Grant Way, Isleworth, Middlesex TW7 5QD; 0171 705 3000

Channel Four Television, 124 Horseferry Road, London SW1P 2TX; 0171 396 444

Cyfle, Llawr Uchaf, Gronfant, Penrallt Isaf, Gwynedd LL5 1NW; 01286 671000

Gaelic Television Training Trust, Sabhal Ostaig, Sleat, Isle of Skye IV44 8RQ; 01471 844373

ITV Network Centre, 200 Gray's Inn Road, London WC1X 8HF; 0171 843 8000

National Council for the Training of Journalists, Latton Bush Centre, Southern Way, Harlow, Essex CM18 7BL; 01279 430009

S4C, Park Ty Glas, Cardiff CF4 5DU; 01222 747444

Publications

It is vital that you stay up to date with who's who and what's what, so always keep an eye on the media pages of the national press (for example, the *Guardian* on Mondays) or, better still, if you can afford it, subscribe to a trade paper. These are some of the more accessible publications:

Audio Visual (monthly; multi-media communications)
Broadcast (the weekly trade paper of the television and radio industry)
Campaign (weekly; advertising)
Media Week (weekly; the advertising, marketing and sales aspects of film and television).
Screen International (weekly)
The Stage and Television Today (weekly newspaper, targeted at actors)
Television (the weekly journal of the Royal Television Society)
Televisual (monthly; production and post-production)
TV World (ten issues a year; international sales and distributions)
UK Press Gazette (weekly; journalism and the media)

For a more detailed list of addresses, please see *Careers in Television and Radio*, published by Kogan Page.

Chapter 4

Crafts

Those who work in the crafts work largely by hand to a high level of skill and design. The objects they produce often have the aim of being both aesthetically pleasing and fulfilling a function. The last 20 years have seen a dramatic increase in art and design HND and Degree trained students opting to work in the craft industries. The traditional distinction between fine art and craft has become blurred. In fact, there has been a recognition in art colleges that students need to be prepared not only to produce craft art but also to manage self-employment and market their products. The Crafts Council estimate that there are 20,000 people working in the craft industries in England and Wales. The spread is not equal: there are more craft workers in the South East, South West and London than in the rest of the country.

Many craftspeople work from their own homes or have a workshop nearby. They live independent lives and enjoy the very direct link between the craftworker and the customer. For example, a furniture maker may well visit a client at home to discuss the design and measurements of a particular piece of furniture. However, it needs to be noted that small businesses have their problems with cash flow and bookkeeping. Seasonal fluctuations in demand may also cause hardship. The Crafts Council found that nearly half of the full-time craftworkers worked for over 50 hours a week, and 23 per cent worked over 60 hours. So, although the profession can be personally and artistically rewarding, it is a tough option.

Qualifications and Training

There are various qualifications open to craftspeople although none is mandatory. Some take degree or diploma courses in Art and Design, and there are City & Guilds trade qualifications.

Some workers are self-taught and others learn from an experienced craftsperson. Individual qualifications will be dealt with under separate craft headings.

Blacksmith/Farrier

Whereas farriers traditionally shod horses, blacksmiths were responsible for producing iron work and agricultural machinery. Blacksmiths are also concerned with industrial smithing in shipyards and the construction of bridges and buildings. Although the terms blacksmith and farrier have become synonymous, blacksmiths cannot shoe a horse unless they are a registered shoeing smith (RSS). Farriers are trained in the art of blacksmiths as well.

Training

Blacksmith. Apprenticeships last three years and are a combination of work with a registered farrier and attendance at a residential course at Herefordshire College of Technology's School of Farriery for 13 weeks in the first year and eight weeks in each of the subsequent years. *Farrier.* To become a farrier it is necessary to register with the Farriers Registration Council. This can only be done following a four-year apprenticeship with a farrier and passing the diploma examination of the Worshipful Company of Farriers.

Further Information

The Farriers Registration Council, PO Box 49, East of England Showground, Peterborough PE2 6GU; 01733 371171

Herefordshire College of Technology, Folly Lane, Hereford HR1 1LS; 01432 352235.

National Association of Farriers, Blacksmiths and Agricultural Engineers, Avenue R, Seventh Street, NAC, Kenilworth CV8 2LG; 01203 696595

The Worshipful Company of Blacksmiths, The Clerk, 27 Cheyne Walk, Grange Park, London N21 1BD; 0181 364 1522

The Worshipful Company of Farriers, White Garth, 37 The Uplands, Loughton, Essex IG10 1NQ; 0181 508 6242

Bookbinder

Bookbinding is the collecting, storing and presentation of printed material. Bookbinding consists of collecting printed matter on sheets, sewing it together on folded leaves and then casing it. There are four principal types of book binding:

- *Trade binding.* Binding pages together in the cheapest possible way.
- *Library binding.* The binding of hardback books and editions by machine.
- *Conservation.* Restoring and preserving old and valuable books and manuscripts.
- *Fine binding* (also known as designer or *craft binding*). This is still done by hand while trade and library binding are done by machine.

This entry concerns itself with *craft binding* and *conservation* work. They involve two main processes called forwarding and finishing. Forwarding is the sewing together of the sheets, the addition of the spine of the book, its backing, and pressing. It is a complicated process producing a perfect, flat, parallel-shaped book. At the head and tail of the spine is an endband which is not only a decorative feature and signature of the bookbinder but also takes the strain when the book is taken from the shelf. The covering process varies, depending on the leather or materials used. It requires skill not to mark the leather in the covering process. Finishing is the decorative process. It can include the application of gold leaf or gold foil, and inlays or onlays of leather. This involves several combinations of materials and techniques.

Bookbinders can work from home. They are likely to work on special limited editions or even just one copy of a book. Customers are likely to be private collectors, antiquarian book dealers or institutions.The bookbinder who specialises in restoration or conservation work will find a great deal of demand from big libraries, county archives and private collectors but will need to set up a workshop. Bookbinders may well join a trade practice, perhaps with a local printer who is undertaking the production of limited editions. Usually, bookbinders find a niche or market which their craft can supply.

Training

There are HND courses in Bookbinding at Croydon College and the London College of Printing (part of the London Institute). Roehampton Institute offers an HND in Calligraphy and Bookbinding.

Further Information

Bookbinding and Allied Trades Management Association, 12 Roy Road, Northwood, Middlesex HA6 1EH; 01923 821037

Ceramics (Potter)

In the previous edition of this book this job title appeared as potter. The field of ceramics is, however, much wider than the term pottery suggests. It includes domestic ware, architectural decorative ceramics and pure sculpture. The difference between the small craftworker and the large commercial producers of ceramics is one of scale. The commercial producer will be interested in batchs of 1,000, the small craftworker in 100 or less.

For the small producer, finding a market for your products can be difficult as there are so many small producers. Some have a shop and workshop combined. Others may find retailers to sell on their unique product. Others may approach customers direct – people who want a small batch of indvidual work, like restaurant owners. Although competition is great, there is always room for a quality product.

Training

Some craftsworkers become apprenticed to Master Potters, but the majority go to art college and take a degree or HND in Ceramics. These are available at: HNDs: Lowestoft College, Staffordshire University, Swansea Institute of Higher Education. Degrees: Bath College of Higher Education, Bretton Hall College of Higher Education, Camberwell College of Art (part of the London Institute), Cardiff Institute of Higher Education, Central St Martins' College of Art, DeMontfort University, University of Derby, Duncan of Jordanstone College, Falmouth College of Art, Loughborough College of Art and Design, Middlesex University, North East Wales Institute of Higher Education, Staffordshire University, University of Sunderland, Surrey Institute of Higher

Education, University of Ulster, University of the West of England, University of Westminster, University of Wolverhampton.

Further Information

Crafts Council, 44a Pentonville Road, London N1 9BY; 0171 278
   7700
The Crafts Potters Association, William Blake House, Marshall
   Street, London W1V 1LP; 0171 437 7605

Furniture Crafts

The last 15 years have seen a marked upturn in the range of furniture manufacturing. There has been a move toward small, efficient, specialised companies producing original items. These small companies have been able to adapt quickly to changes in fashion. They are, however, unable to produce long runs of complicated furniture or spend time on development.

The making of furniture by hand and restoring furniture requires three main skills: cabinet making, upholstery and French polishing.

Training

Courses include: C&G 5550 in Furniture Crafts; C&G 5624/5640 in Upholstery. BTEC National Diplomas will teach some of the skills required. To qualify as a furniture designer there are: *HND courses* in Furniture Design at Basford Hall College, Buckinghamshire College, Manchester College of Art and Technology (also Furniture Design and Craftsmanship and Restoration), Rycotewood College (also Craftsmanship and Restoration), Shrewsbury College of Art and Technology. *Degree Courses* at University of Central England, De Montfort University, Kingston University, Leeds Metropolitan University, Loughborough College of Art and Design, Middlesex University, Shrewsbury College of Art and Technology, Nottingham Trent University, Ravensbourne CDC, (See Chapter 2 for qualification routes.)

Further Information

The Association of Master Upholsterers, Francis Vaughan
   House, 102 Commercial Street, Gwent NP9 1LU; 01633
   215454

The Guild of Master Craftsmen Ltd, 166 High Street, Lewes, East
   Sussex BN7 1XU; 01273 478449

Glassmaker

Glass designer craftsworkers combine a range of skills to produce
decorative glassware in small craft workshops. This involves:

- *Glass blowing.* Forming molten glass roughly into shape by
  blowing down a tube into it while spinning the tube.
- *Serviting/Finishing.* This involves taking the blown material
  and shaping it with tongs, palette knife and wooden blocks.
- *Decoration.* Applying decorative designs using a variety of
  techniques including mitre wheel cutting, engraving, sand-
  blasting and stencilling, acid etching and polishing.

Some glass craftsworkers specialise in stained glass work, restoring old stained glass windows and screens, or creating new
products. It is possible for workshops to have their own small
glass furnace.

Training

Designer craftsworkers will usually have taken a degree in Art
and Design – Glass. These are available at: De Montfort University, Middlesex University, Staffordshire University, University
of Sunderland, Surrey Institute of Art and Design, University of
Wolverhampton. A non-degree course in Glass Technology is run
by Dudley College of Technology. It is aimed at those who wish
to work in a glass studio or set up their own business. It is full
time and lasts 36 weeks.

Further Information

Dudley College of Technology, International Glass Centre, Moor
   Street, Brierly Hill, West Midlands DY5 3EP; 01384 455433.
Glass Training Ltd, British Glass Manufacturers' Confederation,
   Northumberland Road, Sheffield S10 2UA; 01142 661494
Guild of Glass Engravers Federation, 49 Creation Hill, London
   SE1 1XP; 0181 731 9352

Jewellery Design

Jewellery designers create a wide variety of items either by hand or through methods of large-scale production. These may be traditionally styled pieces, using gold or platinum, cheaper costume jewellery, using synthetic stones and base metals, or fashion accessories made from beads, plastic and wood.

A few designers find work developing expensive jewellery, the more costly costume jewellery. The centre for this kind of jewellery is Hatton Gardens in Central London. However, there is more scope for original designers working on an artist/craft basis making fashionable jewellery with semi-precious stones. These may be made to order for a particular store or other outlet, while others make individual items, selling them privately, at craft fairs and to retail outlets specialising in such work.

Training

See Chapter 2 page 11 for **Education for Art and Design**. Jewellery designers will usually take an HND or Degree in Metalwork/Jewellery/Silversmithing. These are available at: HND: Kent Institute of Art and Design, London Guildhall University, School of Gemmology and Allied Studies, Plymouth College of Art and Design, Surrey Institute of Art and Design. Degrees: Buckinghamshire College, Camberwell College of Art (the London Institute), University of Central England, Central St Martins College of Art, De Montfort University, University of Derby, Duncan of Jordanstone College, Kent Institute of Art and Design, London Guildhall University, Loughborough College of Art and Design, Middlesex University, North East Wales Institute of Higher Education, Sheffield Hallam University, Surrey Institute of Art and Design, University of Ulster.

Further Information

British Jewellery and Giftware Federation Ltd, 10 Vyse Street, Birmingham B18 6LT; 0121 236 2657
National Association of Goldsmiths, 78a Luke Street, London EC2A 4PY; 0171 613 4445

Leather Craftworker

A wide range of leather goods are made by mass production methods. However, many jobs in the industry still involve the application of craft skills. Leather craftworkers use many different hand tools. Craftworkers even make their own thread by rolling and waxing hemp. They may make handbags or shoes. One specialised area is Saddlery. Saddle making is still carried out by hand and requires considerable skill. Saddlers often work for one of the many small companies who specialise in saddlery and harness making, and other leather goods such as satchels and wallets. Some saddlers open their own shops where they sell the above items and, generally, suitcases, and offer a repair service.

Most leather craftworkers are self-employed or work for small firms. Many work on their own.

Training

Most leather craftworkers in employment are trained on the job. There are short courses provided by the Rural Development Commission for those already employed in the industry. Cordwainers College in Hackney, East London is the main provider of full-time training in leather crafts. It offers:

College Diploma in Fashion Bags and Travel Accessories
    (two years)
Certificate in Fashion Bags or Light Leather Goods (one year)
Diploma in Leather Craft and Saddlery (two years)
Diploma in Saddlery Studies (two years)

Those who attain the standards set by these courses may apply for the relevant skills tests and submit their work for assessment to the Guild of Master Craftsmen and/or the Society of Designer Craftsmen.

Further Information

Cordwainers College, 182 Mare Street, London E8 3RE; 0181 985 0273
Rural Development Commission, 141 Castle Street, Salisbury, Wiltshire SP1 3TP; 01722 336255

Modelmaker

Almost everything can be prey to the professional modelmaker's craft: towns, oil terminals, palaces, office blocks, hospitals, quarries, shopping centres, cars, ships, planes and so on. Models are often scaled-down versions of the real thing – a planned shopping centre – or they can be enlargements, as in a working model of an atom. Modelling also includes embellishing with gold or silver. The uses that models are put to are legion: a working model of an oil refinery can be used as a test bed before the proper building begins; a model of a new ring road can be shown to those who commissioned it before it is built; a model of a bottle can be tested for its good looks, ease of handling, weight and capacity before it is manufactured in volume. Models are frequently used on television and in films, and also in documentaries and news programmes.

Professional modelmakers work in most towns, many of them specialising in a particular field. One might make working engines, another architectural models and another presentation boats. Some make models for museums, for estate agents' windows, and to be photographed for books and magazines. They may design and make their own models or work on designs supplied by architects or designers. Although there are some freelance modelmakers, it is better to work for a design consultancy first.

Training

Most HNDs or Degrees in Three-dimensional/Spatial design will cover modelmaking. There are, however, some specialist courses in Modelmaking at: HND: Barking College, Bournemouth and Poole College of Art, University of Hertfordshire, Kent Institute of Higher Education, Rycotewood College, Suffolk College. Degrees: University of Hertfordshire and the University of Sunderland.

Stone Mason

Stone masons repair and restore stonework in old buildings and also provide stonework for new buildings, anything from cladding and paving to arches, staircases and fireplaces. The two kinds of masonry work are *banking* and *fixing*. Banker masons prepare the rough stone ready for use in a building and fixers assemble the stone where needed. In large firms, the jobs are separate but in smaller firms a mason may do both.

There are many different types of jobs for stone masons: some specialise in monumental work – making and carving grave-stones; others specialise in particular types of stone – for example, granite or marble.

Training

This is a three-year apprenticeship, supplemented by day release, to attain NVQs awarded by City & Guilds and the Construction Industry Training Board. The Building Crafts College also offers a one-year City & Guilds course in Advanced Stonemasonry which covers stone carving, letter cutting and conservation and restoration techniques.

Further Information

Building Crafts College, 153 Great Titchfield Street, London W1P 7FR; 0171 636 0480
College of Masons, 42 Magdalen Road, London SW18 3NP; 0181 874 8363

Thatcher

Thatchers are self employed craftworkers who thatch houses, pubs, barns and summerhouses with long straw, Devon wheat straw or Norfolk reed. A thatched roof gives good insulation and lasts for 50 years. A roof is thatched by taking off the old thatch and then pegging down new layers of straw or reed. A four-bedroomed house would take a master thatcher and two apprentices about eight weeks to complete.

Training

Academic qualifications are not essential. Thatching can be learned on the job as an apprentice. This takes four to five years and is supervised by a local government training officer or by the Rural Development Commission which also provides a series of short courses to supplement training.

Further Information

Construction Industry Training Board (CITB), Bircham Newton, Kings Lynn, Norfolk RE13 6RH; 01553 776677

National Council of Master Thatchers Association, Thatchers Rest, Levens Green, Great Munden, nr Ware, Hertfordshire SG11 1HD

National Society of Master Thatchers, The Castle, Great Bedwyn, Marlborough, Wiltshire SN8 3LU; 01672 870225

Society of Designer Craftsmen, 24 Rivington Street, London W1R ILH; 0171 739 3663

Rural Development Commission, Training and Productivity Section, 141 Castle Street, Salisbury, Wiltshire SP1 3TP; 01722 336255

Chapter 5

Fashion

When thinking of fashion it is usually clothes that spring to mind. Top designers such as Yves St Laurent, Cacharel and Armani are known by name to many people, few of whom could afford to buy their clothes. There are other designers too, such as Laura Ashley, who are less exclusive and cater for a wider market. Indeed, at the time of writing, London has been hailed as the fashion capital of the world. Fashion is not only dress but where you live, where you shop, where you eat, what sheets you put on your bed, what you order to drink. It may be a colour, a material, a style of make-up or hair.

Most people would agree that fashion starts with design, and that is the area we are interested in here: fashion design and textile design. Fashion design is the design of dresses and accessories. Textile design is the design of dress and furniture fabrics, wall hangings and curtain fabrics. The two are complementary: the fashion designer requires an understanding of textiles and their uses; the textile designer must be aware of how fabrics are used in the clothing and decorative areas.

Qualifications and Training

Fashion and Textile courses exist at all levels of qualification – foundation, vocational (C&G, BTEC National, GNVQ), HND and Degree. The outlines in **Education for Art and Design** (page 11) and **Qualifications and Training** (page 13) described in Chapter 2 apply here. Some courses combine fashion and textile design as the main area of study. The courses involve creative, academic, technical and, increasingly, business aspects. For example, general design studies, professional design studies, professional design practice, techniques such as weaving, printing, dyeing, pattern design and cutting/sewing skills, machine and hand-knitted fabrics and clothes.

There are some courses in fashion and textiles which are solely devoted to one subject for specialised study, for example: embroidery, design of carpets and related textiles, knitwear design. Some courses offer business or management studies, including accounts, commerce and marketing. Others may offer an industrial placement and are offered as sandwich courses. Most designers will have been to art school and have an HND or degree. It is important to realise that no specific level of education is indispensable for, or guarantees, any particular level of job. People with different levels of qualification may do the same job, particularly in small companies. Career progression in the industry is achieved on merit, through experience, as expressed in a strong portfolio of work.

Below are listed the HNDs and Degrees available.

First degrees in Fashion, Textiles and Clothing

First degrees are available at the following universities:

Ulster at Belfast: Dip HE/BA (Hons) Textiles and Fashion Design; BA Fashion Design with Business Studies

University of Brighton: BA (Hons) Fashion Textiles Design with Business Studies

Central Lancashire: BA (Hons) Combined Degree. Creative Design for Fashion

Cheltenham and Gloucester College of Higher Education: BA (Hons) Fashion Design Technology

De Montfort University: BA (Hons) Fashion and Textile Design

Derby: BA (Hons) Fashion Studies

East London: BA (Hons) Fashion Design and Marketing

Heriot-Watt: BSc (Hons/Ord) Clothing; Textiles with Clothing Studies or Marketing

Heriot-Watt: (studied at Scottish College of Textiles, Galashiels) BSc (Hons) Clothing; Textiles with Clothing Studies

Huddersfield: BA/BA (Hons) Fashion with Manufacture, Marketing and Promotion; BEng/BEng (Hons) Textile Management with Clothing Studies

Kent: (studied at Kent Institute of Art and Design, Maidstone) BA (Hons) European Fashion

Kingston: BA (Hons) Fashion and Textiles

Liverpool John Moores: BA/BA (Hons) Textiles/Fashion

London Institute: (studied at St Martin's College of Art and Design) BA (Hons) Fashion Promotion; Menswear; Product Development for the Fashion Industries

London Institute: (studied at the London College of Fashion) BA (Hons) Fashion

Manchester Metropolitan: BA (Hons) Clothing; Fashion; BSc (Hons) Clothing Engineering and Management; Clothing (Marketing and Distribution or Management and Technology); Clothing Marketing and Distribution or Marketing Technology

Manchester (UMIST): BSc (Hons) Clothing Engineering with Management with a Modern Language; Clothing Engineering and.Management

Nene: BSc (Hons) Leather Technology

Northumbria at Newcastle: BA (Hons) Fashion; BA (Hons) Fashion Marketing

Nottingham Trent: BA/BA (Hons) Clothing Studies with Textiles

Nottingham Trent: (studied at Southampton Institute) BA (Hons) Fashion

Southampton: (studied at Winchester School of Art) BA (Hons) Fashion; Fashion/Textiles

West of England, Bristol: BA (Hons) Fashion/Textile Design

Westminster: BA (Hons) Fashion

The following first degree courses are at other colleges:

Bretton Hall College of Further Education: BA (Hons) Fashion (validated by Leeds University)

Colchester Institute: BA (Hons) Design (Fashion Pathways) (validated by Anglia Polytechnic University

Edinburgh College of Art: BA (Hons) Painting, Printmaking or Tapestry (validated by Heriot-Watt University)

Ravensbourne College of Design: BA (Hons) Fashion and Textiles (validated by the Royal College of Art)

Somerset College of Art and Technology: BA (Hons) Design (Fashion) (validated by the University of Plymouth)

Surrey Institute of Art and Design: BA (Hons) Fashion Promotion and Illustration; BA (Hons) Textiles (validated by Surrey Institute of Art and Design)

Sutton Coldfield College: BA (Hons) Fashion and Textiles (Surface Decoration) (validated by De Montfort University)

BTEC Higher National Diplomas in Design (Fashion/Textiles)

Barnet College
Berkshire College of Art and Design (Maidenhead)
Cheltenham and Gloucester College of Art and Design
Colchester Institute
University of Derby
Dewsbury College
Bournemouth and Poole College of Art and Design
De Montfort University
Edinburgh Telford College
Epsom School of Art and Design (options in Fashion, Fashion
    Promotion and Illustration, Millinery)
Kent Institute of Art and Design (Rochester)
The London Institute
Leicester South Fields College
Manchester Metropolitan University
Mid-Cheshire College
Nene College (Northampton)
Newcastle College
Northbrook College (Worthing)
North Tyneside College
North Warwickshire College
University College Salford
Salisbury College
Southampton Institute of Higher Education
York College of Further and Higher Education
Yorkshire Coast College (Fashion/Costume)

The BTEC HND in Business and Finance may be taken with a specialism in Fashion Business at Croydon College or the London College of Fashion (part of the London Institute) or with a specialism in Fashion Retail at the London College of Distributive Trades.

The BTEC HND in Science (Leather Technology) may be taken at Nene College.

A Diploma of Higher Education in Textiles and Fashion Design is offered at the University of Ulster.

Fashion Designer

The fashion designer creates designs for clothes and accessories. Many students specialising in fashion design hope to find work as design assistants in the studios of fashion houses of the well-known *haute couture* firms producing original collections of model garments. Unfortunately, there are few posts in such establishments, many of them being designer owned. If you are lucky enough to be taken on as a design assistant, or more likely as a sketcher, fitter or hand, these *haute couture* houses provide excellent training.

In wholesale *couture,* designers produce original garments but they generally follow the instructions of an employer as far as style and cost are concerned. The wholesale manufacturer must be able to predict what future trends are likely, combine this with the firm's own brand image, match it to available fabrics and create a garment which can be produced economically and will appeal to their particular sector of the market. To do this well, a designer must be extremely well informed and may spend considerable amounts of time researching, visiting shows of fashion collections, talking to buyers and marketing staff, selecting suitable fabrics and looking at portfolios of students seeking jobs.

Some designers work freelance, perhaps producing designs commissioned by clothes manufacturers or designs of their own that they hope to sell to them. Some manage to set up on their own where they design and produce garments on a small scale and sell them through mail order and perhaps a limited number of shops.

Freelances do have scope as to where they live. However, generally they work in-house and must live where the fashion houses are – in London and other world fashion centres.

Salary

The starting salary for a design assistant is around £10-12,000. For an experienced designer, it is £20,000. Top designers will earn £60,000+.

Textile Designer

Textile designers create designs for woven, printed and knitted fabrics, as well as carpets and wall coverings. There are ancillary areas too such as embroidery, lace and trimmings. They work in close conjunction with manufacturers and fashion designers. A good textile designer needs technical knowledge of manufacturing methods, dyes and yarns.

This is a very competitive area in which to find work. In the 1980s, many large textile companies closed down. There are some openings with manufacturers in-house. There are also specialist studios which work for a number of manufacturers.

Some textile designers work as designer/craftworkers, designing and producing their own work for exhibition, direct sale or for specific shops.

Salary

As for Fashion Designer.

Further Information

CAPITB Trust (Clothing Training Board), 80 Richardshaw Lane, Pudsey, Leeds LS28 6BN; 0113 239 3355

Chartered Society of Designers, 29 Bedford Square, London WC1B 3EG; 0171 631 1510

The Design Council, Haymarket House, 1 Oxendon Street, London SW1Y 4EE

The Textile Institute, 10 Blackfriars Street, Manchester M3 5DR; 0161 834 8457

Publications

Drapers Record (Weekly)
Fashion Weekly (Weekly)
Knitting International (Monthly)

Fashion Pages of National Press:

- The *Guardian* (Monday and Saturday)
- The *Independent* (Thursday and Sunday)
- The *Observer* (Sunday)
- *The Times* (Saturday and Sunday)

Chapter 6

Film and Video

Film and videotape are both used to record moving images. The images on film are of a higher quality and, therefore, more suitable for projection on to a cinema screen. Film cameras allow directors more scope than video cameras and so many television commercials are shot on film. Video equipment is cheaper and easier to use. Much of it is light and electronic news gathering (ENG) equipment can be used by one person, making it ideal for news reporting.

The Film Industry

The film industry is located mostly in or around London. It consists of production companies, studios, post-production houses and film distributors.

Production companies, of which there are hundreds around London (many based around Wardour Street), actually develop projects for and make films. They will usually have one or more in-house producer and director, a personal assistant and a messenger. The number of permanent staff is kept to a minimum, with the technical staff for each production being hired on a freelance basis.

The *studios,* such as Shepperton, Pinewood, Elstree and Ealing, do not produce films. They are what is known as 'four walled', letting space and facilities to production companies who usually bring their own crews with them. Some production companies are based at the studio full time and others relocate themselves at the studio when they are using the facilities for filming.

The *post-production sector* of the industry includes the film laboratories and a number of companies who provide editing rooms, film sound recording studios, opticals and special effects.

Film distributors handle the marketing and publicity for films as well as co-ordinating the physical distribution of film prints to cinemas and screening rooms. Most of the staff are clerical.

The Video Industry

Over the last ten years this has been a rapidly expanding sector which is not only London based. It makes features and commercials for television, and a great deal of non-broadcast materials. These include training, point of sale, recruitment and promotional videos. There is a great deal of work in this area. For example, most universities will produce a video prospectus. The set-up is like that of the film industry: there are small production companies consisting of perhaps four full-time employees with an *ad hoc* team of freelances assembled for each production. The growth of this sector offers another 'way in' to the film and television industries.

Qualifications and Training

There are number of HND and Degree courses on offer which relate to the film and television and video industries. (These are listed on page 34 in Chapter 3 on **Broadcasting**.) This chapter covers other training which may be of interest to the reader. There are a number of specific training organisations which should be highlighted here. These are:

The National Film and Television School
This offers a full-time postgraduate course of three years' professional training, enabling graduates to take positions of responsibility in all aspects of film and television production: animation; cinema photography; direction; editing; fiction direction; producing screen design; screen music; screen sound and screen writing. The average age is 25 although there are no rules on this. Candidates need to demonstrate basic skills in their chosen specialist area. Terence Davis, the director of 'Distant Voices, Still Lives', was a graduate of this course at 30. For further information, contact the National Film and Television School, Beaconsfield Studios, Station Road, Beaconsfield, Surrey, Buckinghamshire HP9 1LG; 01494 671234. The school is relocating to Ealing Studios in 1998.

London International Film School

The London International Film School offers a practical two-year diploma course to professional level accredited by the film technicians' union, BECTU. Approximately half of each term is devoted to film production, and half to practical and theoretical tuition. All students work on one or more each term and are encouraged to switch unit roles to experience different skill areas. Facilities include two cinemas, two shooting stages and 15 cutting rooms. Equipment includes 35mm and 16mm panavision, Arrifex and rostrum cameras, Nagra recorders, Steenbeck editing machines and U-matic video. Tuition is by permanent and visiting professionals. Applicants should have a degree in art or technical diploma. Other applications may be considered in the case of special ability or experience. All applicants must present examples of their work. Courses begin in January, April and September. For further information, contact the London International Film School, 24 Shelton Street, Covent Garden, London WC2 9HP; 0171 836 9642.

Scottish Broadcast and Film Training Ltd

This is an employer-led partnership operating in Scotland which provides training for the film and video industries. It operates a New Entrants Scheme that provides 18-month training places across production, craft and creative areas for young people over the age of 18. For further information, contact Scottish Broadcast and Film Training Ltd, 4 Park Gardens, Glasgow G3 7EY; 0141 332 2201.

Skillset

Skillset is the industry training organisation for the broadcast, film and video sectors. Founded in 1992 and recognised by the Department for Education and Employment, it provides relevant training information. Currently, it is setting up a database with the British Film Institute and local Regional Arts Boards of long and short courses available. For further information, send an SAE to Skillset, 124 Horseferry Road, London SW1P 2TX; 0171 306 8585.

Video Engineering and Training (VET)

VET's courses are intended for people with a basic knowledge who wish to update their skills. They include non-linear editing and introduction to video technology. For further information, contact VET, Northburgh House, 10 Northburgh Street, London EC1V 0AH; 0171 430 4001.

Jobs in Film and Video

The various jobs involved in film and video production are, in essence, already described in Chapter 3 which deals with television broadcasting. Here, the unique nature of the jobs in this industry are highlighted.

Camera Team

Other members of this team include the *camera operator* (see page 37); the *focus puller*, who turns the lens and the camera on its mount at the agreed speed and time and assists the camera operator with any special lens or filters and generally looks after the camera; the *clapper loader*, who is the camera assistant, writing up and operating the clapper board, loading films into the magazines and sending used film for processing; the *key grip* who is the leader of a separate team of grips or riggers who prepare tracks, cranes and dollies, and erect scaffolding and platforms for the camera and lighting; and the *gaffer* who is in charge of the electricians who work on a production.

These roles are 'blurred' in smaller productions. In video productions, the director of photography and camera operator are one and the same.

Continuity Person

This is a very important job, making sure that everything, from the position of a prop to clothing to gestures and voice inflections, matches from one shot to the next. The continuity person is responsible for the physical continuity of the film and will work closely with the director. The job requires detailed notes taken on each shot, keeping a detailed log of each day's work including how long each shot took and how many retakes, and notes on what problems occurred.

Working in Arts, Crafts and Design

Director (see page 44)

Director of Photography

The person doing this job may also be referred to as the *cinematographer* or *film lighting camera woman/man*. Apart from the director, he or she is the most creative member of the film production team. Such people work very closely with the director, and are responsible for lighting each shot, choosing camera angles, lenses and filters. They are the senior members of the camera team.

Editor (see pages 39–40)

Producer (see also page 42)

The main difference between the television producer and film or video producer is the latter's duty to secure the finances or commission work. The producer for film and video companies will actually hold the purse strings.

Production Manager

The production manager will be responsible for the overall organisation of the picture under the producer – in effect, the producer's assistant. It is the job of the producer to prepare a detailed budget for shooting during pre-production and a shooting schedule based on that budget. The production manager works closely with the budget manager and director. Once in production, the production manager supervises the smooth running of the shoot, and is responsible for such things as the contracts being completed correctly, the hiring of equipment and obtaining of permission to shoot on location.

Sound Technicians (see also page 45)

On feature films the sound crew is headed by the *sound mixer* who sits at a mobile mixing desk during filming, adjusting levels and tone, as required as they come through the headphones. The other members of the team are: the *boom operator* who uses a telescopic microphone on a mechanical arm or hand held; and the *sound assistant*, who helps them both, and labels and sends off the recorded tapes to the *sound editor*, and keeps a log of takes.

Further Information

British Film Institute (BFI), 21 Stephen Street, London W1 2LN;
0171 255 1444

Broadcasting, Entertainment Cinematograph and Theatre Union (BECTU), 111 Wardour Street, London W1V 4AY; 0171
437 8506

First Film Foundation, 222 Kensal Road, London W10 5BN; 0181
969 5195

Producers' Alliance for Cinema and Television (PACT), Gordon
House, Greencoat Place, London SW1P 1PH; 0171 278 7916

Publications

Books:

The Broadcast Production Guide (International Thompson)
Careers in Television and Radio (Kogan Page)
Careers in Film and Video (Kogan Page)
Kemps International Film and Television Yearbook
Media Courses UK edited by Lavina Orton, published by BFI

Magazines and Journals:

Audio Visual (monthly; multimedia communications)
IMPACT (monthly magazine of PACT – Producers' Alliance for
Cinema and Television)
Screen International (weekly)
Sight and Sound (monthly; BFI)

Chapter 7

Museum and Art Gallery Work

In the last ten years the world of museums and art galleries has changed dramatically. They are now increasingly commercial. Many national and local authority museums and art galleries that were traditionally free have introduced admission charges. Also there has been the advent of slick merchandising by the larger museums. The museum or gallery shop is nearly always the last stop of your cultural experience. This has coincided with the growth of heritage centres and independent and commercial museums. The modernisation of this sector has also had some advantages. Today, museums present information through modern mediums such as video. They use modern technology to make the driest subject engaging. The Science Museum in London has a children's gallery with many interactive displays and games. They have education officers who liaise with schools. There has been considerable investment in making museums and galleries as much a part of the leisure industry as houses of academic reverence.

There are about 3,000 museums in Great Britain. Over a half of these opened in the last 20 years. They range from famous national institutions to local collections housed in library annexes. Of these, around 400 employ 90 per cent of the staff. The collections include everything from museums of industries, coins and medals to dolls and dolls' houses.

There are, broadly speaking, three main categories of museum and art gallery: national; local authority; and others belonging to a particular society, university or private organisation. The national museums and galleries contain the most important national collections and are financed and maintained by the government. These offer the most scope for the traditional academic specialist curator. These curators may combine collection management with departmental management. National museum curators are usually graduates in a discipline relevant to their department. They are likely to start off as assistant curators.

Local authority museums and art galleries make up 1,000 institutions. They include some large, prestigious centres and hundreds of small museums representing local history or culture, such as the People's Palace in Glasgow.

The largest group are the independents which are funded by sponsors or by entry fees. These are entertainment led. Usually, they employ the most sophisticated technology to bring their educational mission alive. Good examples are the Museum of the Moving Image in London or the Yorvik Viking Centre in York. Jobs in this sector are likely to go to those with commercial skills as well as specialist knowledge. These are organisations run for profit rather than public good.

Other museums, such as the Ashmolean in Oxford or the Fitzwilliam in Cambridge, draw their funds from the universities or societies that have set them up. Jobs in this sector are more likely to be taken by the traditional 'academic'.

Conservation and restoration professionals are also employed in museums and art galleries to preserve and make good the paintings and artefacts.

Both local authority and independent museums use a great deal of volunteer labour. This kind of voluntary experience can be invaluable when applying for jobs in this highly competitive area.

Qualifications and Training

A good degree is usually necessary to become a curator. The suitability of the subject may depend upon the position being applied for. There are no first degrees for Museum and Art Gallery Studies as a separate subject. There are, however, some which include such studies and provide periods of study in a museum or art gallery. These are: University of London/Courtauld Institute of Art's History of Art; University of Leeds' History of Fine and Decorative Arts; University of East Anglia's Art History; and De Montfort University's History of Art and Design.

There are also degrees in Museum and Heritage Management. These include Heritage Management at Cumbria College of Art and Design, and Heritage Conservation at Bournemouth University. There are specific qualifications at postgraduate level for museum and art gallery work. These are one-year, full-time. The most renowned and long-established of these is Leicester University's Diploma in Museum Studies. The University of Manchester has a Diploma or MA in Art Gallery and Museum Studies, which emphasises art gallery work. The University of Newcastle upon Tyne and University College London both offer an MA in Museum Studies. The University of St Andrews has a Diploma in Museum/Gallery Studies and the Courtauld Institute an MA in Art Museum Studies.

There are also courses run by Sotheby's, Christie's and the Study Centre for Decorative Arts which may be relevant for entry into the profession.

Almost all those involved in conservation or restoration will undergo full-time training before entering work. These courses will specialise in one subject or material. Examples include: sculpture, furniture, paintings, ceramics and textiles. A complete list of Training in conservation is available from The Conservation Unit, 16 Queen Anne's Gate, London SW1H 9AA; 0171 233 4200. There are also archaeological conservation courses offered by the University of London and the University of Wales at Cardiff.

Education officers employed by museums and galleries should have both teaching and museum qualifications.

Design staff have relevant art and design qualifications (see Chapter 2).

Jobs in Museums and Galleries

Conservationist/Restorer

Conservation staff have the task of cleaning, maintaining, repairing and restoring objects or works of art to their best condition. These include paintings, prints, textiles, fossils, statues, arms and armour, furniture, machinery, metalwork and paper. Most of the large galleries have their own laboratories for this purpose. Their first task is to prevent damage: this involves daily care, and attention to the conditions under which items are displayed. The effects of temperature and lighting change must be considered.

Conservation staff must also examine and record the objects in their care. Many objects have to be treated to prevent deterioration. This may involve complex processes which must also be carefully documented. The aim of conservation is to preserve objects from further deterioration or damage; the aim of restoration is to restore objects to their original appearance while keeping their historical integrity.

Curator

Curators are responsible for the administration of the collections under their care. They are often helped by assistant curators/keepers. In larger museums and art galleries, a curator's duty may involve the management of a laboratory and the supervision of conservationists and restorers. The mounting of new exhibitions is a part of a keeper's job, plus overseeing the publicity material and catalogues that accompany such exhibitions. The curator is responsible overall for the administration of the museum's funds. Some curators devote time to research and may be acknowledged experts in their own field.

The work of the art curator is very similar. However, there is a much greater emphasis on the selling of works of art and engaging the buying public.

Designer

There are a few opportunities for designers, mainly graphic and three-dimensional. Designers mainly concentrate on the design of displays and exhibitions. Graphic designers may also produce publicity material. They generally work under the supervision of the professional museum/gallery staff. They may also work with modelmakers (see page 57) and photographers who, as freelances, may be employed to take pictures of collections or to set exhibitions in context. Some studio technicians may also be employed to deal with the technical aspects of display and design work such as mounting and dressing displays.

Education Officers

Education officers, also known as schools service officers, are employed by national museums and galleries to liaise with teachers in organising lectures and demonstrations as well as school visits and lessons held on the museum or gallery premises.

Further Information

Association of British Picture Restorers, Station Avenue, Kew, London TW9 3QA; 0181 948 5644

Association of Independent Museums (AIM), Hotties Science and Arts Centre, PO Box 68, St Helens, Merseyside WA9 1LL; 01744 22766

Museums and Galleries Commission, The Conservation Unit, 16 Queen Anne's Gate, London SW1H 9AA; 0171 233 4200

The Museum Association, 42 Clerkenwell Close, London EC1R OPA; 0171 608 2933

Museum Training Institute, Kershaw House, 55 Well Street, Bradford BD1 5PS; 01274 391056

The National Association of Decorative and Fine Arts Societies NADFAS House, 8 Guildford Street, London W1N 1DT; 0171 430 1730

The United Kingdom Institute for the Conservation of Historic and Artistic Works (UKIC), 6 Whitehorse Mews, London SE1 7QD; 0171 620 3371

Chapter 8

Photography

Photography remains one of the purest forms of communication. Its great advantage over the written word is that it does not need to be translated for use in another country and, placed in context, speaks for itself. Its applications are myriad. In medicine it is used for research, investigation, documentation and as a teaching aid. Newspapers and all forms of publication rely heavily on photographic images. Crime detection and investigation involve the use of both simple and highly sophisticated photographic techniques such as ultra-violet light shooting. There are industrial and scientific photographers who may use high-speed photography to find a fault on a machine which moves faster than can be seen by the human eye. There are also the prestige areas of fashion or advertising photography which employ small numbers of people but give us a particular image of the photographer in the studio. Finally, there are the general practice studios which employ approximately half the professional photographers in Great Britain and will traditionally take wedding or portrait pictures.

It is still unclear how professional photography will be affected by the advent of electronic imaging. This can now be used by designers to manipulate photographs and create new images. The new technologies can also accurately represent or simulate images for research.

The greatest opportunities for employment lie in those industries connected with amateur photography – photographic manufacturing, retailing and photofinishing; the greater prestige and competition for jobs is within the professional field – advertising, fashion and press.

Photofinishing laboratories, both for the public, and professionals, provide a number of job opportunities. The laboratories processing film for the general public mainly offer machine-minding and maintenance jobs. The professional laboratories still allow considerable scope for skilled work. It is possible to work in many fields of photography to work anywhere in the country, for example, in general practice (or High Street photography), police, medical, scientific or industrial. However, for the perceived glamorous jobs in fashion or advertising and national newspapers, it is essential to be based in London. These photographers are usually employed on a freelance basis.

Below are described some of the possible qualifications and routes (such as they are) into professional photography. Whatever the level of qualification achieved, it is most likely that the would be photographer will start his or her career as a photographer's assistant. This requires very mundane tasks to be undertaken such as setting up equipment, loading film, setting up lighting, organising transportation of equipment, dealing with paper work, etc. This is very much an industry in which you have to pay your dues. In some cases photographers may prefer to take on a young person with a keen interest and flexible attitude to be their assistant rather than a trained college or art school graduate.

Qualifications and Training

There are many photography courses available at all levels. There is, however, no formal progression from training to employment. The general education for photographers follows the format described in Chapter 2 in **Education for Art and Design** (page 11) and **Qualifications and Training** (page 13). As stated above, formal qualifications may not always be required for entry into the profession. Assistants without qualifications may take the City & Guilds 747 or NVQ as a day-release course.

Other qualifications include:

BTEC National or GNVQ Advanced Diploma in Art and Design (Check with local colleges or Careers Service)

Higher National Diplomas in Photography at: Berkshire College of Art and Design, Bournemouth and Poole College of Art and Design, Bradford and Ilkley College of Art and Design, Carmarthenshire College of Technology and Art, Dewsbury College, Leicester Southfields College, Mid Cheshire College, Newcastle College, St Helens College, Sandwell College of Further and Higher Education, Stoke on Trent College, Swansea Institute of Higher Education, Tameside College of Technology

Higher National Diploma in Photography – Advertising, Fashion, Editorial at: Kent Institute of Art and Design, Wigan and Leigh College

Degrees in Photography at: Blackpool and Fylde College, University of Central England, University of Derby, Falmouth College of Art, Kent Institute of Art and Design, Northbrook College, Nottingham Trent University, University of Northumbria, University of Plymouth, Staffordshire University, University of Sunderland, Surrey Institute of Art and Design, Swansea Institute of Higher Education, University of Wolverhampton

Degrees in Photography – Advertising, Fashion, Editorial at: University of Brighton, Cleveland College of Art and Design, Kent Institute of Art and Design

Specific training qualifications are dealt with below under the appropriate job titles.

Advertising and Publicity Photographer

This type of work is highly specialised, demanding and competitive. Although it can fall into the province of the general practice and freelance photographer, the mainstream and most lucrative contracts will be beyond their resources. Generally, such assignments will go to highly esteemed photographers, who have experience in a particular field, and who have well-equipped photographic studio facilities. Usually, work is provided by an advertising agency (see Chapter 1).

Advertising is, by nature, a competitive field and agencies are always on the look out for photographers who can produce pictures which are original and stunning. They aim to attract customers' attention, to show the desirability and superiority of the product. The subjects can vary enormously from cars to food. The pictures may also be used in a variety of media including brochures, posters, newspaper advertisements, etc. The scope for creativity may be quite small as the advertising agency will provide a specific brief from an art director as to the image required. This may be given as a sketch or written. If the photographer has the ability to put an extra 'spin' on the image, this will make for a successful career. In this field the photographer must be a team player, able to take instructions from the art director and work with models, stylists, lighting technicians and agency staff.

Fashion Photographer

Fashion photography is all about style and showing clothing, shoes, hats, stockings, underwear and make-up to the best possible advantage. To be successful in this area the photographer needs to take pictures that are distinctive and portray the kind of image and style which the art director wants to communicate. The photographer has to be able to portray the human form and garments in a way which makes them highly desirable.

A good temperament, personality and motivational skills are vital to success in this area as much of the work involves bringing the best out of the model in the studio, and other team members. For a shoot, photographers may have to employ make-up artists or hair stylists as well as lighting technicians and the trusty assistant. They may also choose and book their own models.

Organisational skills are therefore essential to ensure successful completion of an assignment.

All fashion photographers work freelance. Very rarely they may work under contract to a large client. There are two basic categories of fashion photography: *location* and *studio*. Usually a photographer will do both. Unless very well established, a photographer will hire studio space by the day as this is much cheaper. They may even hire an assistant for the day. Photographers will often hire their equipment too, as good basic equipment could cost £5–£10,000 and different work requires different equipment. However, most photographers still carry a lot of their own equipment.

Work is usually for magazines, advertisements and promotions and is provided by an agent who will make all the business arrangements, usually for a 25 per cent fee. Most top fashion photographers started by being assistants to other top fashion photographers.

Further Information on Advertising and Fashion Photography

The Association of Fashion, Advertising and Editorial Photographers, 9–10 Domingo Street, London EC1Y 0TA; 0171 608 1441. This organisation will put photographers and assistants on its books and act as agents for assistants.

Industrial Photographer

Industry employs a considerable number of photographers. These can either be in-house or freelance. In a highly technical industry, photography may be used as part of quality control and the detection of faults in manufactured goods. This may be in the form of high-speed photography or using close-ups.

Photographers may also be involved in taking photographs for company brochures, publicity material or in the compiling of instruction handbooks. Many local authorities employ photographers to cover civic events or work in their publicity departments.

General Practice Photographer

This is the term given to photographers with premises in towns – sometimes known as High Street photographers. They specialise in photographs of weddings and other social occasions, such as christenings and graduations. They may offer portraiture, particularly of children. Some may pick up work from local companies and agencies. A general practice photographer may also be asked to take some press photographs for the local newspaper. Many general practices have their own processing and developing laboratories. Employment opportunities vary and some positions offer no more than being a basic shop assistant.

Science Photographer

There is some overlap between this work and the work of the industrial photographer. The difference is that the scientific photographer's work is used to provide information essential to research in a scientific or engineering field. At times, the scientific photographer will be required to work in controlled conditions of particular temperature or humidity. He or she will also need to keep extremely detailed notes on the progress of work and the prevailing conditions at the time. People entering this field require a high level of technical ability and possibly some training in engineering. Science photographers often work for the Civil Service, in private industry and for universities.

Medical Photographer

Many hospitals have photographic departments. This is to satisfy clinical, research, publication and teaching requirements. Medical photographers must photograph injuries, operations and post mortems. They must be able to deal with nervous or ill patients and not be squeamish.

Medical photographers must keep abreast of new techniques and must be conversant with video and film photography and closed circuit television. They must become expert at techniques such as macrophotography, endoscope photography and the use of infra-red and ultra-violet light sources. Long-term projects may be undertaken under controlled conditions. The photographer may also be responsible for producing teaching and training aids. Medical photographers generally start as trainees.

Training

Trainees in hospitals gain experience on the job and usually study for the medical photography exams of the British Institute for Professional Photography or the Institute of Medical and Biological Illustration. It is also possible to enter after taking a full-time specialist course.

Further Information

Institute of Medical and Biological Illustration, 27 Craven Street, London WC2 5NX

Police Photographer

The majority of photographers in the police force are civilians. The work involves: copying finger prints, photographing stolen items and recording injuries. Often the photographer is one of the first called to the scene of a crime or accident. In addition, he or she may be required to produce materials for police training programmes.

Police photographers do their own developing and are expected to keep detailed paperwork on individual photographs which may be admitted in court as evidence.

Specialist photographic techniques, such as macrophotography and photomicrophotography, are required to record and compare textile fibres, dust, hair, handwriting and typescript. Infra-red techniques may be used to examine blood stains or powder burns and to detect fake paintings. The work is essentially to keep a faithful record of evidence or events.

Further Information

Police Recruitment Department, F5 Division, Room 516, Home Office, 50 Queen Anne's Gate, London SW1H 9AT; 0171 273 3353

Press Photographers

The press photographer must have a good 'eye' for news and be able to interpret a story and rapidly take advantage of the best opportunities to take a picture. The art of summing up a complicated situation with a single photograph is their trade. In competition with television, the national dailies require the ability to come up with an original 'take' on a situation or event that is already in the public domain. Most photographers, however, will start with local newspapers where the requirement is for material of regional and human interest. This often means photographing a lot of mundane events such as village fetes and civic openings. The good photographer will add something extra and build up a strong portfolio of work.

The transition from local to national newspapers is subject to intense competition. In the national press the work is much more news orientated. The pressure of deadlines is greater as is the need to produce a picture which is better than your rival's.

Only highly reliable, talented and resourceful photographers make this difficult transition. The work can be tough and dangerous. On overseas assignments the photographer may have to cope with poor living conditions, physical and mental stress and the extreme difficulty of getting pictures from remote locations to the newspaper to meet a deadline.

There are a number of other job titles in the area of press photography. These are:

Agency Photographer

Some news and press agencies employ their own photographers. This job is similar to that of a staff press photographer.

Editorial Photographer

Editorial photography is used to illustrate and accompany information in magazines, periodicals and technical journals. Generally, the photographer is freelance, and often specialises in one or more subjects.

Photojournalist

Photojournalism is the art of telling a story with pictures. Magazines and Sunday supplements take some material of this kind. The work is freelance and the market small.

Training

There are two main schemes of training. These are: *direct entry* to a training contract with a local or provincial newspaper. Direct entrants receive on the job training and block release to Sheffield College. A one-year full-time *pre-entry course* is organised by the National Council for the Training of Journalists at Sheffield College which requires candidates to have a minimum of four GCSEs/SCEs at grade C or above and one A level. Freelance photographers do not have to have completed these courses.

Further Information

National Council for the Training of Journalists, Latton Bush Centre, Southern Way, Harlow, Essex CM18 7BL; 01279 430009

Other Employers of Photographers

Photography is also available as a career option in: the *Civil Service*, mainly for the Ministry of Defence, where strict rules apply to nationality; and in all three branches of the *Armed Services*, where application to photographic duties can be made after entry.

Further Information

Recruitment and Assessment Services, Alencon Link, Basingstoke, Hampshire RG1 1JB; 01256 29222 (Civil Service)
Local forces recruitment centres – see Yellow Pages

Photographic Technician

The majority of opportunities in photography are for technicians in photofinishing and professional laboratories. Photofinishing companies process the films made by the general public and are generally concerned with producing large quantities of prints with a fast turn-around time, hence one-hour developing. The jobs in this sector can often involve routine machine minding. Professional laboratories may cater for specialist needs, although the tasks undertaken are broadly similar. These are listed below. A technician may be required to perform them all or may specialise in one part of the process depending on the working environment.

Processing. This is done by machine and is automatically controlled. The technician is, however, responsible for testing, setting and adjusting the machine as well as sorting and loading the films.

Printing. This is mostly done by machine for both amateur and professional films.

Hand Printing. This may be done where there is a particular requirement from the photographer, for example an enlargement of part of a picture.

Finishing. Prints may be requested to be mounted on hardboard for display or to have a sepia effect, or a particular surface texture.

Duping. The technician here makes exact copies of a transparency. Sometimes the duplicate has to be larger than the original. This involves rephotographing the original on to a special duplicating film and requires great care to be taken to ensure sharp focus, filtration and exposure.

Copying. This involves using a special camera to copy a photograph or piece of artwork for which there is no negative and producing a negative.

Retouching. This is a highly skilled job and requires considerable artistic expertise. When prints are imperfect and have blemishes, retouchers will remove them. In the case of advertising photographs, they may remove unwelcome features that distract from the central image using airbrushes and paint brushes. They may also change original colours.

Electronic Imaging. This is used to manipulate images. It involves converting the image into a computer image which can then be altered or merged on screen, the final image being converted back to a photographic form.

Training

This is usually on the job. Those entering this profession will usually start as trainees or juniors doing the more routine and repetitive jobs. There are NVQs available in Supporting Photographic Processing Operations, Processing Photographic Material, Printing Photographic Material and Electronic Imaging. It is also possible to study a full-time BTEC National Diploma in Photography and Photographic Practice at Kingsway College London (two years). It is estimated to take three years to become professionally competent. However, the new technologies will mean that regular further training will be necessary.

Further Information

British Institute of Professional Photography, Fox Talbot House, Amwell End, Ware, Hertfordshire SG12 9HN; 01920 464011

Kingsway College, The Grays Inn Centre, Sidmouth Street, London WC1H 8JB; 0171 306 5700

Photography and Photographic Processing Industry Training Organisation, 44 George Street, Reading RG3 2RL; 01734 590816

Professional Photographic Laboratories Association, 35 Chine Walk, West Parley, Ferndown, Dorset BH22 8PR; 01202 590604

General Further Information

British Institute of Professional Photography, Fox Talbot House, Amwell End, Ware, Herts SG12 8HN; 01920 464011 (please send an A4 envelope with 29p stamp)

The Association of Photographers, 9 Domingo Street, London EC1 0TA; 0171 608 0598

Publications

Where to Study, British Journal Directory of courses in photography, film, video and television

Design Courses, Design Council

Beyond the Lens, Association of Photographers

The British Journal of Photography (weekly)

Chapter 9

Printing

Printing is one of Britain's largest industries. There are over 6,000 firms in the UK, employing over a quarter of a million people. Printers do not only produce newspapers and magazines but also help to produce wallpaper, floor coverings, bank notes, stationery for computers and even plastic cash and credit cards. Printers will tend to specialise in a particular kind of work, as each end product requires slightly different presses and folding, and binding and gluing processes.

The main specialisations in the industry are:

- General: High Street printers
- Books
- Colour printing: cards, brochures, art reproduction
- Newspapers
- Security printing: bank notes, bonds, credit cards
- Cartons: for the food and retail industries
- Magazines
- Labels
- Stationery
- Print on metals: beer cans, etc

Because of the expense of equipment for different techniques, companies will often also only specialise in a single part of the printing process. This may be in the preparation stages of printing: typesetting, layout and platemaking; or the finishing processes of cutting, stapling and binding. There is a future in printing despite the advances in technology. For although this has meant that some of the processes require less skilled craftworkers, it has also increased the possibilities and hence the demand for printed materials. The craftworker 20 years ago has been replaced by computer control of the production process. The work now calls increasingly for technical skills.

Qualifications and Training

There is the full range of qualifications in printing. These are listed below:

City & Guilds
Craftworkers are almost always trained on the job. The City & Guilds is often denoted as an NVQ.

BTEC National Diploma
See *Directory of Further and Higher Education* published by CRAC/Hobsons.

BTEC Higher National Diploma in Printing
London College of Printing and Distributive Trades (LCPDT), Manchester Metropolitan University, Nottingham Trent University, Watford College, West Herts College. BTEC HND in Business and Finance may be taken with a specialism in Printing Management at the LCPDT.

First Degrees
Herriot Watt University, Manchester Metropolitan University, Reading University, Wolverhampton University

The British Printing Industries Federation conducts exams annually in: Estimating; Introduction to Printing Technology, Sales and Print Order Processing. It offers a Certificate in Printing Administration covering the above subjects and exams are taken in two stages. Management wishing to take these courses can do so through correspondence courses, or attending a college of further education.

The LCPTD is the specialist college for the industry and is a part of the London Institute from craft to postgraduate courses.

For **Bookbinding** courses, see page 52.

Jobs in Printing

Keyboard Operator

Today most type-setting is done by keyboard operators. They use large typewriters with additional functions. The customer or designer passes the text to the operator and they discuss the design requirements, such as typeface or layout. Operators may also be required to make their own decisions on design and text.

Make-up Compositor

The make-up compositor makes up the page to its final design using the copy and illustrations passed on by the keyboard operator. This usually involves cutting and trimming the copy to the required size so it fits the page design. It is then fixed into place with adhesive, ready to be photographed.

Camera/Scanner Operator, Planner and Platemaker

Camera operators photograph the original of a drawing or photograph and from this produce a negative or positive image as required. This is passed to the *planner* who lays it according to the number of pages. A lithograph plate is then produced from which the final print is made.

Electronic scanners are increasingly used for colour processing as separate film and plates do not have to be produced for each colour (as with cameras), and the colour separation is done automatically. These require less skill on the part of the operator. *Platemakers* expose the plate with the negative or positive image to ultra-violet light in a vacuum frame. They will also process the plate to reveal the image and remove any blemishes. This can also be done by a *retoucher*.

Machine Printer

They set up the machines for the final printing of the product. There are many different types of machine and so many techniques, according to the printing process involved. The task is to transfer the image to paper, plastic or board. They will usually use control consoles. In larger organisations, they will have print assistants to help them. They will check the consistency of the printing and adjust the machines appropriately.

Binding and Finishing

The processes of this function are described in Chapter 4. However, in the industry this is mostly machine handled.

Office Jobs

There are other 'office' jobs in the print industry. These are: *departmental managers* who run the offices; *order clerks* and *account executives* who look after individual printing jobs, writing instructions and checking the product's arrival and departure from the department; *estimators* who work out how much jobs will cost; *sales staff* who find customers; and *design staff* who may also be employed on a freelance basis (see **Graphic Designer**, Chapter 2, page 21).

Further Information

British Printing Industries Federation, 11 Bedford Row, London WC1R 4DX; 0171 242 6904

Institute of Printing, 8 Lonsdale Gardens, Tunbridge Wells, Kent TN1 1NU; 01892 38118

London College of Printing and Distributive Trades (part of the London Institute), Elephant & Castle, London SE1 6SB; 0171 514 6500

Scottish Print Employer's Federation, 48 Palmerston Place, Edinburgh EH12 5DE; 0131 220 4353

Society of Typographic Designers, The Cottage, Chapelfield, Randwick, Stroud, Gloucestershire GL6 6HS; 01453 759311

Chapter 10

Publishing

Publishing is an industry rather than a profession. It is a relatively small industry employing around 20,000 people. The largest area of employment is in general (or trade) publishing. This includes fiction and non-fiction, adult and children's books, sold in hard covers and paperback, by shops, through book clubs or by mail order. There are also specialist publishers who work in a specific subject area which provides a guaranteed market. These include: educational publishers; publishers of dictionaries, encyclopaedias and reference books; fine art publishers; and fine binding (limited edition) publishers. Many older publishing houses will combine trade and specialist publishing.

Book publishers are increasingly exploiting the possibilities offered by the electronic media: the conversion of books into a form combining text with image, sound and video on CD-ROM (Compact Disc-Read Only Memory). The CD-ROM can present an enormous amount of information and mix media information which the reader can easily access. It has had its greatest impact in the area of educational and reference materials which are enriched by this form of presentation.

Publishing houses may differ in their structure and organisation, but most have three main departments:

- Editorial
- Production/Design
- Sales and Marketing

Editorial Department

Editor

More applicants are attracted to this department than to any other, although editors make up a very small percentage of the labour force. The editorial function is divided between acquiring the manuscripts and preparing them for publication. The *acquisitions* or *commissioning editor* (also known as sponsoring editor or publisher) is required to find authors or books of quality. This type of editor is market orientated. This means being alert for ways to expand a particular market. It may involve buying the rights to already published titles or commissioning translations of foreign titles. The commissioning editor will need to find new writers, encourage writers who are going through an unproductive period and retain writers who may be sought by rival publishing houses. He or she will negotiate and maintain contact with literary agents to ensure that good work is offered.

The *editors* have the closest contact with authors. They need to read widely and be aware of buying trends and current events. In liaison with other departments, the editor takes the accepted manuscript through the various stages to deliver a bound book within a specified timeframe at an agreed price. Within these constraints, editors always work to deadlines and stress is an occupational hazard. The editor works with the minimum of supervision and is responsible for maintaining his or her own deadlines and budgets, passing page proofs for production, and approving jacket copy.

Desk editors (also known as sub editors, or copy editors) read a manuscript and check it for copyright illustrations or passages, and prepare it for the printer by ensuring consistency of content and style. Their job is also to check references and facts (where there are doubts) and correct grammar, spelling and punctuation mistakes. They may discuss with, or suggest to, the author revisions, picture content, design and production schedules, choose the illustrations, and draft the jacket blurb and catalogue copy. Once the manuscript has been edited, it will be designed ready for production. When the text has been set in type, the editor sends proofs to the author (proof reading one set in-house) and then collates the two sets of corrections and returns the proofs to the printer for correction at the next stage of production.

The desk editor may also be responsible for compiling or updating entries for directories and encyclopaedias from data supplied.

Editorial assistants are the beginners in the department. They will work under the supervision of a senior on tasks such as desk editing, the preparation of captions for illustrations, chronologies, bibliographies, listing names to appear on maps for the cartographer or artist to work from, checking indexes, researching bibliographical information, updating books for new editions, obtaining pictures and so on.

Picture Research

Picture research is a professional wing of the editorial or art department in those companies that publish illustrated books. The researcher will be provided with a list of pictures or subjects which are required for a book and a copy of the manuscript, briefed on the format and design, and then asked to provide an agreed number of suitable photographs. The researcher needs a knowledge of copyright relating to illustrations and the ability to work within a budget. The picture researcher will need to know the cost of a print, and the cost of reproduction charged by the copyright holder and reconcile this with the requirements of the title and its budget.

Production Department

The production department is responsible for the manufacture of the books. Its function is to ensure that the titles are produced to the highest standards available for the agreed price and within a specified time. Designers may be under editorial supervision but are usually attached to the production department with their own manager or director.

Production Controller

In larger publishing houses there are teams consisting of an editor, designer, production controller, and sometimes a picture researcher working on their own series or list of titles. The production controller will check that the submitted manuscript is of the length agreed and will draw up a specification for the production of the book. With a knowledge of printers, paper suppliers and binders, the production controller will decide which companies should be invited to provide estimates for the work. When the best prices have been achieved, the controller will add in the known in-house expenses to come up with the production estimate. The editor will then use this to estimate the final cover price of the title after adding a mark-up for trade discounts, the publisher's gross profit and the author's royalty. If this final figure is too high, the team discusses how savings might be made. The production controller then places the orders for typesetting, machining (printing) and binding, and ensures that all the production stages are carried out to the required standard and on schedule.

Since this department spends more than any other, the production manager needs to have financial acumen, technical knowledge and the ability to administer and organise effectively. There are also production assistants who enter publishing in a trainee capacity, or as an administrator, designer or stock controller and decide to train for production at day or evening classes while undertaking undemanding production work such as reprinting.

Designers

Designers in publishing are usually part of an art department which works closely with production. In small publishing houses there may be just one department and sometimes one person responsible for production and design. The work involves all aspects of book design – layout, typeface, type sizes, style and arrangement of illustrations, jacket or cover. The design must be within the limitations of available production services and acceptable costs. The designer's work also includes the preparation of layouts, sketches and specimen pages and dummies. The *design manager* or *director* co-ordinates and oversees all these activities as well as commissioning freelance artwork. This department may also produce publicity leaflets, catalogues and company stationery.

Sales, Marketing and Publicity

The main function of the sales department is to sell books and rights. To this end, its marketing and publicity sections are responsible for the pre-publication research, preparation of catalogues, price lists, leaflets, posters, display stands, and all other sales aids. They are also responsible for the advertising and promotion of the product, for sending out review copies and obtaining the maximum free publicity possible. This work involves liaison with editorial, production and design staff.

This section keeps records of sales and customers, and works with the accounts department checking credit worthiness and credit control. The sales director is in charge of this department and will have a thorough knowledge of the trade both in the home and export markets. Usually, he or she will have started as a homes sales representative with defined territories, working from home, taking repeat orders and selling new titles. Some representatives call on schools and colleges rather than bookshops and are known as educational representatives.

Marketing and publicity are under the control of a *marketing manager* and a *publicity manager,* sometimes the same person. As mentioned above, it is their job to obtain as much free publicity as possible. As margins are too low for regular advertising of each individual title, they will look for free editorial coverage arising from reviews, press releases, literary prizes and authors' book-signing sessions. Marketing staff may also try to build up mail order lists, particularly if the house has specialised titles.

Other Jobs

Rights manager In small firms this job is done by the editor. The rights manager sells the rights to titles which are owned by the publisher. These often include English Language rights, paperback right and United States rights.

Large, well-established firms may also employ a **copyright and permissions editor** who deals with requests from individuals and other publishers to reproduce passages from books to which that particular house has rights.

In the accounts departments there are **royalties clerks** who calculate the royalties due to the author, once or twice a year depending on the contract.

Literary agents work separately from publishers, acting as the brokers of an author's work to publishers, film producers and theatre companies. Sometimes they will also act for foreign publishers attempting to find a British publisher who will bring out an English edition of the book. They, like publishers, will specialise in fiction, non-fiction or specialist publishing.

Qualifications and Training

Publishing companies are notorious for the lack of formal training opportunities, and often rely on 'learn as you go' training, usually supported by more experienced colleagues, particularly for editorial skills. A far wider range of training options has, however, become available in recent years. In particular, the advent of desk-top publishing has led to a multitude of new short courses which include the production of newsletters and promotional catalogues. An example is the range of courses set up by Middlesex University Small Press Agency aimed at self-publishers.

There are also short courses provided by various colleges for those already employed by publishing companies. These include: Copy Editing, Production Skills, Layout and Print Buying, On-screen Editing, etc. One of the main providers of such courses is the Book House Training Centre, the Industry Training Organisation for publishing.

Below are listed the specific full-time courses available in publishing under the job title headings:

Most **editors** are graduates of some discipline. There are, however, specialist courses available as follows:

HNDs in Publishing/Publications
Blackpool and Fylde College, Farnborough College, Gloucestershire College of Art and Technology, Napier University

Degree Courses in aspects of publishing
Loughborough University, Luton University, Napier University, Oxford Brookes University, Robert Gordon University, Thames Valley University

Postgraduate Diplomas
The London College of Printing, Middlesex University, Plymouth University, Stirling University, West Hertfordshire College

Post Graduate Higher Degrees
Middlesex University, Plymouth University, Stirling University

Production Staff (also see Chapter 9 for qualifications and training in printing)

Designers will normally have undertaken a HND or Degree course (see Chapter 2, page 13, **Qualifications and Training**). There are some specialist courses as follows:

HND in Typography
Cleveland College of Art and Design, Edinburgh's Telford College, London College of Printing, Stafford College, Stockport College of Further and Higher Education, West Herts College

Degrees in Typography
University of Plymouth, Reading University

Degree Courses in Graphic Media Studies with options in publishing
Hertfordshire University, West Hertfordshire College

Postgraduate Diploma (Narrative Illustration)
University of Brighton

Further Information

Book House Training Centre, 45 East Hill, Wandsworth, London SW18 2QZ; 0181 874 2718
London College of Printing, Elephant and Castle, London SE1 6SB; 0171 735 0810
Middlesex University Small Press Agency, White Hart Lane, London N17 8HR; 0181 362 6058
Publishers' Association, 19 Bedford Square, London WC1B 3HJ; 0171 580 6321
Careers in Publishing and Bookselling (Kogan Page)

Chapter 11

Teaching

Teaching may be entered as a first choice profession, or after an art and design degree. It offers a vocation in its own right as well as a second string to the artist who may have other ambitions. There are opportunities for teachers in primary schools, secondary schools, adult education, further education and higher education. Of the total art and design students graduating in 1996 (7,460) around 5 per cent went on to teacher training. To teach in further, adult and higher education, it is not always necessary to have a teaching qualification, although it is desirable.

Approximately 550 art and design teachers are trained every year for secondary schools. These teachers may work in art and design or craft designs and technology (CDT) departments. There are also opportunities to work as general teachers in primary schools, specialising in art and crafts. It may also be possible, after appropriate experience, to qualify as an **Art Therapist** (see Chapter 2, page 27). Teaching is a portable qualification which can be used anywhere in the country and even abroad.

Qualifications and Training

To train as a teacher in state or grant maintained schools requires a minimum of five GCSEs/SCEs at grade C or above (which must include English Language and maths). Those who enter initial teacher training for primary school teaching after September 1998 will also be required to hold a GCSE at C or above in science (or equivalent).

1. A Bachelor of Education (BEd) course or BA/BSc with Qualified Teacher Status (QTS).

Usually requiring two A levels or appropriate Access qualification for entry. Applications for these courses must be made through UCAS, PO Box 28, Cheltenham, GL50 3SA; 01242 222444

2. A Postgraduate Certificate in Education (PGCE) which is studied after a first degree for one year.

This may also be entitled the Postgraduate Art Teachers' Certificate/Diploma (PGATC). It is worth noting that at the time of writing a mandatory grant award is still available from local authorities to study for this qualification. Applications for these courses must be made through the Graduate Teacher Training Registry (GTTR), Fulton House, Jessop Avenue, Cheltenham GL50 3SH; 01242 544788.

For both these qualifications there are specialisms to teach art and design or design and technology. The institutions offering these are listed in Table 2. It may be noted that some institutions offer specialist courses for teaching in further education. It is not essential to have a teaching qualification to work in adult or further education (50 per cent do). It is also possible to study for the part-time City & Guilds 7307/7306 in Further and Higher Education. See the *Directory of Further Education* published by the Careers Research Advisory Centre for details.

Personal Qualities

Teachers need not only artistic talent but the ability to communicate their knowledge clearly and in an interesting way. It is essential that teachers maintain high levels of motivation and organisation as they work alone, without supervision. They must be adaptable enough to teach a range of abilities and be satisfied by the process of gradually developing students. It is a career which requires both physical and mental stamina.

Salary

School teachers are paid according to their qualifications and experience on a salary scale ranging from £12,000–£32,000. Further education lecturers are paid from £12,000–£21000 at the basic grade, rising to a potential £48,000 at management grades.

Table 2 *First degrees and postgraduate certificates in education in teaching art and design*

Art/Art & Design/Creative Arts	BA/BEd		PGCE		
	Primary	Secondary	Primary	Secondary	Further Education
Anglia Polytechnic University				*	
Bath College of Higher Education				*	
Bishop Grosseteste College	*				
Bolton Institute of Higher Education					*
Bradford and Ilkley Community College	*				
Bretton Hall	*			*	
Bristol University				*	
Canterbury Christchurch College				*	
Cheltenham and Gloucester College of Higher Education				*	
Chester University College	*		*	*	
Chichester Institute of Higher Education	*				
De Montfort University	*	*	*	*	
Edge Hill University College (Ormskirk)	*				
Goldsmiths College (UCL)	*	*		*	
Lancaster University	*				
Leeds Metropolitan University		*		*	
Liverpool Hope University College	*				
Liverpool John Moores University	*			*	
LSU College of Higher Education	*		*	*	
Manchester Metropolitan University	*			*	
Middlesex University	*			*	
Nene College	*				
Newman College	*				
North East Wales Institute of Higher Education	*				
Nottingham Trent University	*				
Roehampton Institute of Higher Education	*			*	
Trinity College, Carmarthen	*		*		
University College of St Martin, Lancaster	*		*	*	
University College, Scarborough	*				
University of Brighton	*			*	
University of Cardiff	*			*	
University of Central England	*				
University of Exeter	*			*	
University of Greenwich				*	
University of Leeds			*		
University of Liverpool			*		
University of London (Institute of Education)				*	
University of Plymouth	*			*	
University of Reading	*			*	
University of Wales (Bangor)	*			*	
University of Wales (Cardiff)	*			*	
University of Warwick	*			*	
University of West of England in Bristol	*				
University of Wolverhampton	*				

	BA/BEd		PGCE		
Art/Art & Design/Creative Arts	Primary	Secondary	Primary	Secondary	Further Education
Westminster College, Oxford	*				
Worcester College of Higher Education	*				

	BA/BEd		PGCE		
Design and Technology	Primary	Secondary	Primary	Secondary	Further Education
Bath College of Higher Education				*	
Bolton Institute of Higher Education					*
Bretton Hall				*	
Brunel University		*		*	
Chelthenham and Gloucester College of Higher Education				*	
De Montfort University				*	
Edge Hill University College	*	*			
Goldsmiths College	*	*		*	
King Alfreds College		*		*	
Lancaster University	*				
Leeds Metropolitan University		*		*	
Leeds, Trinity and All Saints	*	*	*		
Liverpool John Moores University		*		*	
Loughborough University		*		*	
Manchester Metropolitan University		*		*	
Middlesex University				*	
Nottingham Trent University	*	*		*	
Open University				*	
Ripon and York St John	*		*	*	
St Mark and St John	*	*		*	
Sheffield Hallam University		*		*	
Swansea Institute of Higher Education				*	
University of Bath				*	
University of Brighton	*	*		*	
University of Central England	*				
University of Exeter		*		*	
University of Greenwich		*		*	
University of Huddersfield		*		*	
University of Leeds			*	*	
University of Leeds (Trinity and All Saints)	*	*	*		
University of Northumbria		*		*	
University of Sunderland	*	*			
University of Wolverhampton	*	*		*	
University of Wales (Bangor)	*	*			
University of Wales (Newport)		*		*	
University of Wales (Swansea)	*				

Further Information

Careers Research Advisory Centre (CRAC), Hobson's Publishing, Bateman Street, Cambridge CB2 1LZ; 01223 464334

Department for Education and Employment, Sanctuary Buildings, Great Smith Street, London SW1P 3BT; 0171 925 5000

Department of Education for Northern Ireland, Teachers' Branch, Waterside House, 75 Duke Street, Londonderry BT47 1FP; 01504 319190

General Teaching Council for Scotland, 5 Royal Terrace, Edinburgh EH7 5AF; 0131 556 0072

Open University, Walton Hall, Milton Keynes MK7 6AA; 01908 274066

Teacher Training Agency (TTA), Information Section, Portland House, Stag Place, London SW1E 5TT; 0171 925 5882

Publications

Careers in Teaching (Kogan Page)

Handbook of Initial Teacher Training in England and Wales National Association of Teachers in Further and Higher Education (NATFHE) (Linneys ESL)

Also publications from the Teacher Training Agency (address above)

Chapter 12

Theatre

It is fitting that this book should end with the theatre as it is an industry which employs the widest range of those involved in the arts, and includes the individual as a conduit of art in the form of the actor. You can get some idea of the range of jobs by looking at the National Theatre whose three theatres under one roof employ over 600 staff, 120 of whom are actors. The rest include: producers, directors, designers, casting directors, musicians, make-up artists, wardrobe managers, production managers, props specialists, stage technicians, electricians, as well as those people who deal with the box office, management, sponsorship and marketing of productions. While many of these jobs are merged in smaller theatres and are done by one person, at the highest level they are career areas. To gain some insight into the business it is well worth visiting the National Theatre which runs daily tours (except Sundays).

Qualifications and Training

Qualifications are not always as important as experience in the theatre and training is often on the job. There are often no formal qualifications for some jobs in the theatre (eg producer). The opportunities for training, where it exists, are listed under the job headings as are the personal qualities required.

Actor

The stage is an overcrowded and heart-breaking profession. Equity, the actors' union estimates that at any given time half its 45,000 members are *resting*. When they are working it is usually on short-term contracts. Hours are long and unsociable. Actors spend most of the day rehearsing and then have to appear in evening performances. Often they are away on tour. The money is only good for top actors.

Equity rates are £190 per week outside London and £225 per week in the West End. It is a profession for the dedicated.

Qualifications and Training. While it is possible to enter the profession without formal training, the National Council for Drama Training (NCDT) advises that a recommended course of training be completed. There are 17 drama schools which are accredited by the NCDT and these are all included in the Conference of Drama Schools prospectus.

Box Office

The box office is in charge of ticket sales – at the theatre, by post and through agents. It may operate the traditional system of crossing off seats on a seating plan, or have a computerised system. The box office manager may also be involved in accounting, promotion and marketing. Experience of accounts and ticket selling are useful first steps to a manager's job.

Casting Director

This is a job found in large companies, television and films. As its name suggests, it involves working with producers and directors, choosing a cast for productions. Casting directors often freelance and are hired for a particular show.

The casting director keeps a record of who has done what and is a natural target for agents who are trying to get work for their clients. Casting directors go to drama school productions to spot new talent. They will be expected to know who is available and draw up lists for the director to choose from. They will arrange auditions and work out the contractual arrangements with the actors and their agents.

Designer

The sets and costumes for a production are sometimes divided between different designers (especially if they are on a large scale), but usually the same designer is responsible for both. The designer will work closely with the director and lighting designer. Often these three individuals will work as a team on a number of productions if they have established a rapport.

Normally, designers are employed for the season or to work on one particular production. They are expected to produce drawings of the sets and costumes for the scenery and wardrobe departments to work from, and a scale model of the sets which will be shown to the cast at the first rehearsal when an outline of the set is chalked on the floor for the actors' guidance until the set is ready.

Stage designers need a thorough knowledge of period settings and costumes, a sense of style and of what will look exciting on stage. They must also have the ability to work within a budget and be able to adapt to a variety of stages from the traditional proscenium to the theatre in the round.

Training. There are courses in Theatre Design/Set Design at:
HND: Central School of Speech and Drama, City College Manchester, Coventry University, Croydon College, London College of Fashion, Newcastle College, Northbrook College (Sussex), North East Worcestershire College;

Degrees: University of Central England, Central School of Speech and Drama, Central St Martins College of Art and Design, Nottingham Trent University, Rose Bruford College, Welsh College of Music and Drama, Wimbledon College of Art.

Director

This is the most creative job in the theatre, as the director has overall responsibility for the artistic side of the production – directing the actors and co-ordinating the backstage and technical departments. The director interprets the piece and will put his or her own stamp on the production. Good directors will often be as big a draw as the play or the actors. Theatre-goers will always be interested to see a Peter Hall *Hamlet* or a Jonathan Miller *Figaro*.

By the very nature of the job, directors have strong personalities and can be abrasive and temperamental. As the 'ideas' people of the theatre, they have to sell their interpretation to the company and shape the production during rehearsals. Once the play is open, the director's job is finished and there is not long to achieve it – eight weeks at the National Theatre, four weeks in commercial theatre.

Training. Some directors begin as actors or stage managers. There are not many training opportunities, some get the chance to act as assistant directors. There are courses at: Central School of Speech and Drama, Drama Studio London, East 15 Acting

School, Mountview Theatre School, Rose Bruford College, University of East Anglia, Welsh College of Music and Drama.

Education Officer

Many theatres have theatre-in-education companies, or employ someone to set up similar schemes with schools and colleges through workshops, talks and backstage visits. They may also arrange school performances to fit in with examination studies and supply actors and technical staff to advise on school productions. This may be an attractive career option for drama graduates with some teaching experience.

House Manager

The house manager is responsible for looking after the theatre and its day-to-day running. This involves ensuring that the cleaning, catering and security arrangements run smoothly and seeing that everything to do with the comfort and safety of the audience is attended to. The house manager is on duty throughout the performance and is expected to deal with any complaints or problems that arise.

Training. The job does not necessarily require any special training or qualifications. Experience as a senior usher or assistant house manager may be useful. Study at higher education level for **Arts Administration** (see Chapter 2, page 28) may also be an advantage.

Press Office

Dealing with the press is only one of the jobs of this very busy department which is responsible for everything to do with publicity. Press office duties might include: priming journalists to write favourable articles; persuading reluctant directors and actors to be interviewed; commissioning photographers for publicity shots for display and handing to the press; ensuring theatre critics receive complimentary tickets. All this needs to be planned well in advance.

The department has to produce a wide range of publicity from posters, advertisements and mailshots to throw-aways, cast lists and programmes. Today, the most simple programmes include photographs and biographies of all the cast. At the top end of the market they include substantial background information, including the history of the production. Tact, self-confidence and a pleasant voice are useful assets when dealing with the press, radio and television.

Training. There is no specific training. However, arts graduates with an interest in media and administration skills may be suited to this career.

Producer

This is a job that occurs in the commercial theatre. In subsidised companies this role is taken by an administrator or executive director. The producer shoulders the responsibilities of putting on a production. This includes choosing the play, renting the theatre, engaging the director and cast and being responsible for paying the bills. The producer has to raise the money to put on the production and decide when to close it.

Training. There is no specific training to be a producer – some are ex-actors. Usually they have been involved in the business for some time.

Production Staff

Large companies, such as the National Theatre and the Royal Shakespeare Company, can afford to have their own production workshops, each with its own speciality. Similar jobs exist in opera and ballet companies, and in film and television.

Armoury. Here weapons are made and mechanical special effects such as gunfire or shells, and decorative metalwork props such as candelabra. Team members will be trained specialists such as gunsmiths or leather workers.

Metal workshop. All the heavy steelwork needed for shows is designed and made here by fully qualified fitter-welders.

Carpentry workshop. Technical drawing as well as carpentry skills are needed here. In smaller theatres outside contractors will be hired.

Paint workshop. This is where the sets are painted. It requires fine art skills to produce the right effect and texture of scenery that may be needed, for example, to represent scenes in Ancient Rome.

Props workshop. Props may be bought or borrowed; sometimes, however, they will be made in the workshop, in particular those used for special effects, such as collapsing chairs, or pictures that fall off walls. It may involve the collection and cataloguing of items.

Wardrobe, wigs and make-up. Although costumes are often hired from a theatrical costumier, a large number are made by wardrobe departments. Costume making requires a good knowledge of period fashion.

Training. There are degree courses in Costume for the Performing Arts at Bournemouth and Poole College of Art and Design and the London College of Fashion; and in Costume Design and Wardrobe at Rose Bruford College. There are also courses at the Bristol Old Vic Theatre School, Oldham College and Wimbledon School of Art. These courses will include some make-up, although it is possible to enter via the hairdressing route. Some colleges run specialist Theatrical Make-up courses.

Stage Manager

The stage manager is responsible for organising rehearsals and ensuring that performances run smoothly. A stage manager usually has several assistants, known as ASMs (assistant stage managers) and in large companies a deputy. The job requires a gift for handling difficult, temperamental people with firmness and tact, an ability to keep calm in a crisis, a good eye for detail, a good memory and, above all, a sense of humour. In small companies, ASMs are sometimes asked to play small parts or understudy, and in the past this has been a first step towards full-time acting.

It is the job of the stage management staff to see that actors know when they are needed for rehearsals and, if necessary, to give them a personal call. Rehearsals are organised in consultation with the director and careful notes have to be made of any script changes. All the moves and actions of the cast, and all the cues for scene changes, sound effects and lighting need to be recorded. One of the jobs of the ASMs is to act as a prompt both in rehearsals and performances in case actors forget their lines. It is also the ASM's job to make sure that all the props are available and to arrange costume fittings for the cast.

In a large theatre like the Opera House the stage manager will be in charge of very sophisticated equipment. The technical box at the back of the auditorium will have an intercom system that allows the stage manager to talk to the lighting director, sound technicians, musical director and ASMs in the wings. When the front-of-house manager arrives to give the OK and the actors are ready, the stage manager will start the action and raise the curtain.

Training. Entry is usually as an ASM for which there are no minimum qualifications. Most applicants have completed a drama school course or have a degree in drama or theatre studies. For more details, see the Conference of Drama Schools Prospectus (available from the NCDT, address below) or contact the Association of British Theatre Technicians (ABTT).

Stage Technicians

Lighting Designer. The theatre electrician may be in sole charge of the lighting, but a large theatre with sophisticated equipment will have a lighting team headed by an expert who will design a lighting plan for the production. The team will rig the lights, operate them during the performance and deal with any technical problems. Lanterns are positioned to create effects and pinpoint actors. In modern theatres the lighting plan will be fed into a computer.

Sound Technician. The job of sound technician ranges from occasional sound cues to providing music if there are no live performers, electronic effects and solving acoustic problems. The advent of the rock musical has meant that there has been a cross over of talent from those trained in the record industry into the theatre.

Training. This may be via drama school stage management courses which include Lighting and Sound. City of Westminster College offers a one-year course in Lighting and Sound which was evolved with the Association of British Theatre Technicians.

Further Information

Association of British Theatre Technicians (ABTT), 47 Bermondsey Street, London SE1 3XF; 0171 403 3778

Conference of Drama Schools, Central School of Speech and Drama, Embassy Theatre, Eton Avenue, London NW3 3HY; 0171 722 8183

National Council for Drama Training (NCDT), 5 Tavistock Place, London WC1H 9SN; 0171 387 3650

Stage Management Association, Southbank House, Black Prince Road, London SE1 7SJ; 0171 587 1514

Index

Suggested Further Reading

The Kogan Page Careers in... Series:

Accountancy *(6th edition)*
Architecture *(4th edition)*
Art and Design *(7th edition)*
Banking and Finance
 (4th edition)
Environmental Conservation
 (6th edition)
Film and Video *(5th edition)*
Journalism *(7th edition)*
The Law *(7th edition)*
Marketing, Advertising and
 Public Relations *(6th edition)*
Medicine, Dentistry and Mental
 Health *(7th edition)*
Nursing and Related Professions
 (7th edition)
Police Force *(4th edition)*

Publishing and Bookselling
 (2nd edition)
Retailing *(5th edition)*
Secretarial and Office Work
 (7th edition)
Social Work *(6th edition)*
Sport *(6th edition)*
Teaching *(6th edition)*
Television and Radio *(6th edition)*
The Theatre *(5th edition)*
Travel Industry *(5th edition)*
Using Languages *(7th edition)*
Working Outdoors *(6th edition)*
Working with Animals
 (7th edition)
Working with Children and Young
 People *(6th edition)*

Also Available from Kogan Page:

Creating Your Career, Simon Kent
*Great Answers to Tough Interview Questions: How to Get the Job You
 Want* (3rd edition), Martin John Yate
How to Pass Graduate Recruitment Tests, Mike Bryon
How to Pass Numeracy Tests, Harry Tolley and Ken Thomas
How to Pass Selection Tests, Mike Bryon and Sanjay Modha
How to Pass Technical Selection Tests, Mike Bryon and Sanjay Modha
How to Pass the Civil Service Qualifying Tests, Mike Bryon
How to Pass Verbal Reasoning Tests, Harry Tolley and Ken Thomas
*How You Can Get That Job!: Application Forms and Letters Made
 Easy*, Rebecca Corfield
How to Win as a Part-Time Student, Tom Bourner and Phil Race
Job Hunting Made Easy (3rd edition), John Bramham and David Cox
The Kogan Page Guide to Working in the Media (2nd edition), Allan
 Shepherd (ed.)
Manage Your Own Career, Ben Bell
Preparing Your Own CV, Rebecca Corfield
Readymade Job Search Letters, Lynn Williams
Test Your Own Aptitude (2nd edition), Jim Barrett and Geoff Williams
Your First Job (3rd edition), Vivien Donald and Ray Grose